AFTER THE LIBERATORS

A Father's Last Mission,

A Son's Lifelong Journey

by

WILLIAM C. MCGUIRE II

1999

Parkway Publishers, Inc.
Boone, North Carolina

Library of Congress Cataloging-in-Publication Data

McGuire, William C., 1943-
    After the liberators : a father's last mission, a son's lifelong journey / William C. McGuire II.
        p. cm.
    Includes bibliographical references and index.
    ISBN 1-887905-19-7
    1. McGuire, William C. 2. World War, 1939-1945--Aerial Operations, American. 3. Bombardiers--United States Biography. 4. United States. Army Air Forces Biography. 5. McGuire, William C., 1943- 6. Fathers and sons--United States--Biography. I. Title.
    D790 .M432 1999
    940.54'4973—dc21
                                                                99-32505
                                                                CIP

Cover Design by Tun Aung and Bill May, Jr.
Editing by Patty Wheeler
Layout and Book Design by Julie Shissler

This book is dedicated to
Matthew Maron,
the missing
and all those
who miss them still

"How long, how long will men remember
Not us who died - - but Why?"

Capt. Robt. J. Hearn, C. SS. R.
Chaplain, U.S. Army
"We Are the Dead"

Invocation

Is the voice chosen or does it choose?
What voice? Which voice?

There can only be one, and it was there even before the void. And long before it gave a name to the light.

You won't find this voice in Genesis, but nonetheless it was there. Before any ear could take it in. Before the dawn of comprehension, the Garden and the Fall. It was there.

Through only some of them, it speaks to all of them. And even these cannot possess it. It is simply in them and with them, for a time. From time to time some hear its music. They are compelled to tell, to witness.

Whether men remember or recognize it or not, it is the first sound they hear and it will be the last, and the lasting. They hesitate to reach for it in fear it will not be there when they most need it. But it has its own reasons. Hearing it once again, speaking through them, the force of it is so sweeping that there is no room for gladness or consequence. Only to witness, to burn with its fire, to cry out in the wilderness, make straight the way of the Lord!

Hearing it, there is no hesitation. They are not afraid. They listen and proclaim. The voice tells them, even in the darkest hour, together we will find the way. So listen now to the truth that echoes through the ages, and rejoice, for peace and glory are at hand.

AFTER THE LIBERATORS

Name of the Father
Prologue

It was, he told himself, as hot as a spring day could be. Leaving the dark marble coolness of French Hospital and stepping into the bright sunlight of the city streets, he was both dazzled and almost overcome by the sudden waves of heat. He fell into an aimless but time-killing stroll that eventually led him around the perimeter of the Penn Station construction site. The magnificent old building was now reduced to a street-level pile of rubble and isolated broken columns. Excavation was beginning on the lower levels.

Office buildings and a new Madison Square Garden would rise up here over a modernized railroad depot, it was claimed. As a native New Yorker, however, he knew enough to view the dismantling of any landmark, or in fact anything that worked, with suspicion. It was a strangely sad scene, in his mind analogous to a desecrated graveyard memorial.

Earlier that morning, he had helped his wife down to the street from their apartment and hailed a cab on First Avenue that quickly took them uptown and across 29th Street to the hospital. He got her as comfortable as he could while she kept reassuring the both of them. But then the rough and ready nurses threw him out of the room to begin to prep her. He protested, rambling on about Lamaze. "We know all about it," they said, waving him away. "Go on. Take a walk. Come back in an hour."

He remembered that huge French woman in the grainy educational film he and his wife had seen together with many other parents-to-be at Lenox Hill Hospital. How she completed her delivery, and then got off the table herself and ambled down the hall like she was on her way to the market. He and his wife were pioneers of sorts in New York. There were only two hospitals in the city that allowed husbands in the delivery room. Now, walking in Herald Square, he wasn't so sure being a pioneer was such a great idea.

Later, he was back at his wife's side timing the still widely separated contractions. Her doctor said she was only a few inches dilated, but that everything was fine. He worried she was getting tired, and he felt more and more frustrated that he couldn't do anything for her pain. The doctor, a big, good-natured woman with a matter-of-fact way about her, stood at the foot of the bed and gripped the railing. She smiled warmly at her patient, tossed her car keys in the air and catching them announced that she was going to dinner.

If this was a trick, it worked, for twenty minutes later his wife was in delivery. He watched from behind her head, rubbing her shoulders and mopping her brow. The head came. And then he could see the baby slip out into Dr. Spalding's experienced hands. A boy, she announced. He kept his eye now on both the child and his wife. He saw the nurses handling him. The afterbirth came. But there was a silence in the room. The lanky infant made no noise, but lay limp and gray in other arms. He was just a few feet away from the both of them but it seemed a barrier that was holding everything back.

The doctor continued to work on his wife and to talk to her calmly, only giving an occasional command to the nurses with firmness but no apparent alarm. His heart was caught in his throat. They pinched the baby and tapped him. "He's too comfortable," the doctor said. On her instruction they quickly immersed him in a bath, and only then did their son awake with a cry. Then came a yawn.

The mother and father smiled, even as tears rolled from their eyes.

Washed and dried, the infant was lain on his wife's breast for the first time and he saw them meet, upside down, and he put a finger in the little fist. Then they let the father hold him. They had their first born, he thought. The Navigator had a grandson who would also carry his name. It was May 30, 1966. Memorial Day.

The memory of that spring day rapidly receded from my mind, and gradually my son's profile came into sharp focus before my eyes. He was as prone as possible on the air terminal molded plastic seat, head back, eyes closed, arms folded across his chest. From our front row seats, his long legs stretched out before him, almost meeting the building's glass outer wall. Outside, the black squall was beginning to break up in patches of lighter grays. The rain stopped and the winds that drove the storm were suddenly determined to be off for some other destination. Lightning flashed for the last time.

It was Friday, August 29, 1997, Labor Day weekend and also my wedding anniversary. Thirty-one years had gone by since that birth day in French Hospital. My son, a man now, a big man, was there next to me, proof of time's passage. He had had a bad headache and his girlfriend, Suzie, had gone off in the car hunting for some painkillers. The terminal waiting room was crowded near the windows that looked onto the field with some seventy-five people. They were mostly couples in their sixties and seventies, their adult children, grandchildren, and great-grandchildren. Some press, radio and television news crews were also part of this unusual gathering. Charged fragments of conversation drifted to us from behind. The planes had taken off from New Jersey and should make their approach in five or ten minutes. This time the rumors sounded convincing and the chemistry of anticipation began to build. Beyond the glass, the clouds unzipped to reveal their blue lining as many pairs of eyes scanned the horizon just over the trees on the airfield's perimeter.

My son stirred. He was feeling more like himself and began to prepare his video camera. We were in the terminal of the old Republic Aviation field on Long Island and it was our ties to the Navigator, my father, that had brought us to this place, once a center for fighter plane manufacturing during World War II. I was one of a baker's dozen of winners of an essay contest on a local radio station, sponsored by the Genovese drug store chain. Entrants were asked to tell about the veterans in their life and why their contributions were significant. I wrote about my son who served in the Coast Guard in Saudi Arabia during the Gulf War. And, I wrote about his grandfather, a B24 navigator shot down over Germany and killed in WWII.

The contest prize was a ride for two on either a B24 or a B17. I lobbied hard for the B24 and was fortunate to get my wish. Like any contest, there had been real competition for the seats on these planes and now there were winners and losers among the spectators.

The crowd began to push through the glass doors and to press up against the low fence leading to the tarmac. As we joined them it was, once again, a lovely day. There was a collective stir as a Flying Fortress came into view flying parallel to and just above the tree line on the edge of the field to our right. Her sleek cigar-shaped fuselage was dressed in the dusky brown of the early war years in the European theater. Descending, she briefly vanished behind the trees, and then, visible once more, touched down, huge among the many parked private and commercial small craft scattered on the fringes of the field.

Above her roaring engines, now only seventy-five yards away, I directed my son to the trees once again. There was the rounder, heavier-looking, double-finned silver silhouette of the "All American" B24 J. Someone called excitedly behind me, "There's the Liberator."

The official for the drug store company began to shout off names from a clipboard and the passengers each responded with a military "Here." The "Lib" swept down and made first contact with its wheels, a metallic-sounding noise that is unlike any other. Then she eased her nose gently onto the runway. She turned and taxied behind the B17, both planes coming to a stop near the gate. But their props continued to spin noisily and impatiently. There would be no engine shut down, we learned.

We seven passengers left the noisy crowd behind and made our way to the whirring propellers of the B24. We entered aft through the camera hatch, my son boosting me up while someone pulled from above. Four riders were already seated on a kind of bulkhead bench just forward of the waist windows, open cut outs for the machine gun placements. We sat on the floor, our backs against another low metal bulkhead wall. My son was on my left, with another guest, a radio reporter, on my right.

Snapped into safety belts, we were hardly settled when we were off and making our way down the runway. My boy was tall enough to continue to tape record through the waist windows from a sitting position as we taxied toward take off. I stared back through the tail gun's plexiglass shield, where the sun cast warm shafts of light in the narrow gloomy darkness. When we were in position for take off, the decibel level revved up and off the charts, and the more than fifty-years-old Liberator's 1.25 million individual parts began to rattle in unison.

Then we were off the ground and rising. Flying. My son let out a war whoop and I yelled above the engines, "Rock and roll!"

Once clear of the field and while we were still gently ascending, our young crew chief host gave us the freedom of the ship and everyone unbuckled. Leaning on the starboard waist fifty caliber gun, I looked out on graveyards, golf courses, and the packed suburbs of Long Island as we leveled off at about 2,000 feet. We flew on a southerly course toward the ocean beaches and then west along the shore line. Bathers and sun worshipers looked up from the sand at us and the 17 on our wing. My eyes were wet with tears. I made excuses to my video man. "So much emotion," I said. Why? Why was it all so important to me, so powerful? But the strongest feeling just then was a heady happiness, a sheer exhilaration despite the tears, and I pushed aside the questions and reveled in the moment with my son.

The two of us, my son trailing with the camera running, went forward, past where the ball turret used to be and down onto the narrow catwalk of the bomb bay. On both sides, dummy bombs were locked in position like fat ribs in the belly of the ship. Below my feet the Atlantic glistened darkly through long slots on either side of the skinny metal track.

The cockpit was crowded with curious passengers. We slid down beneath them into the even tighter confines of the nose, where bombardier and navigator once worked together like a couple of wrestlers in a steamer trunk while enemy flak and fighters created deadly mayhem all around them. Forward was the plexiglass nose, the famous bombsight, the bombardier's control panel, the nose turret above the nose cone. Now I was between the nose wheel and the hatch, alongside my dad's old navigator's work station. The battery light flashed a low power warning on my son's camera. The rest became a kind of blur.

On the ground again, after a half-hour or more, the two of us posed alongside the fuselage for a souvenir photo with a volunteer WWII Army Air Force reenactment group. Thumbs up everyone, and smile! I still have the print. It is a good picture.

After thanking our hosts, we slowly walked back to the spectators on the other side of the gate. As I swung the lock back into position, a man in his sixties said more at me than to me, "And what outfit were you with?"

Was he questioning my right to be there, and to have flown in the Liberator? My first impulse was to just let it go. But I stopped and slowly turned. It could have been an honest question – let's face it, I don't exactly look young anymore. Or, it could have been a neutral one. But something else was in his tone of voice. "My father, his grandfather," I said to the man's profile as I grabbed my son's arm, "was a navigator in the 392nd over there." As I began to move away I added, "And he's buried over there." "Oh," the older man said.

He got the message. Still, I should have kept my mouth shut. But I couldn't help feeling glad I hadn't. On this day, at this moment, I had no tolerance for fools, old or young, and I certainly was not about to be the butt of an inappropriate one-liner.

It seemed that for a good part of my life, I had been explaining or keeping quiet about things that had been kept from me, or were discomfiting or elusive and beyond my understanding. Just go along with this. Don't ask about that. It is all for your own good. But it wasn't for my good. None of it in the end was for me. The habits of youth became part of the man, however. I tried to get along without what was missing in my life but eventually I came to really understand who I was. And with that and some gift of grace, I was at long last able to find my father and reclaim a larger part of myself.

In a way, we came home together. And he flew with us on that flight of the "J" over his native New York. And he walked across the tarmac with his boys. Home again. Yes, home again.

How could such a thing be? How could an otherwise levelheaded fifty-four-year- old man lay claim to such a fanciful possibility? To understand you would have to go where my father and I have been. You would have to hear both our voices tell what they know, each in his turn, until eventually the two become one. It is a story of a strange and wonderful journey, a high arching song of birth, death, and regeneration. And love. Above all the melodic line is love.

To truly follow and understand, you would have to go back to the beginning, to a cold late winter morning in 1944, before the sun came up and the Liberators took to the skies.

Book I
Delayed Action

He was awake.

He didn't know why.

He'd been dreaming of the mission. What was it? The last one. The day before yesterday, wasn't it? He began to play it back, how they went into Southern Germany just above the clouds, lots of clouds. Getting thicker. And flak. Swiss flak or German flak? An interesting question. Couldn't see the Lake, couldn't see the ground, Germany. Couldn't see a thing. The secondary's no good either and they all turned back home. Bombs and all. He figured, looking back, either they couldn't find the 392nd with their fighters or it was one of the those days when the Luftwaffe gets real stingy as they meditate on a coming Allied invasion. A cake walk for the group, or so it seemed, he told himself. Just a few holes in the bucket from shrapnel. Counts for thirty missions, though. But he also knew they would probably change that again too, "Sure as shootin'. And every one we miss we'll only have to go back for, sooner or later." He spoke the words softly to himself. "Probably sooner."

His thoughts turned to the time. Then to the temperature. It was too cold. The dark outline of the stove betrayed its icy contents. All he had to do was lift his arm and turn his wrist but he really didn't want to know the hour. He didn't want to move. He told himself, we will go up this day; it will start any minute now.

The weather? Listening to the sleet and hail striking the Nissen's corrugated roof, he knew it was awful. But it is awful most every morning and that tended to have little effect on whether they would fly or not. Ten hours or so later over the Continent, he knew it would be another kettle of fish, weather or not.

He is navigator on a B24 Liberator, what he described as a fat-bottomed, ungainly-looking heavy bomber, normally manned by a crew of ten. This crew had been together for a little less than a year. It seemed somehow longer to him. He felt it was a good crew and a good ship - - temperamental, but ultimately as reliable as her majestic wing spread and four powerful engines suggested. He told himself it could fly further, faster, with more explosive power than any B17 Flying Fortress, the more numerous European Theater of Operations Eighth Air Force counterpart. With their pilot, Bill Sharpe's skill, their thorough training, and fifteen missions experience, he knew they were a potent combination. Together, they had decided to name their recently acquired B24 J model "Sinister Minister," but they hadn't been able to coerce a painter into properly labeling #100117 yet.

Still unmoving in the cot he mused: "March in merry old England, cold like a knife to the bone." But nothing like 23,000 feet, now that was cold. He heard steps and caught the outline of the door in the corner of his eye as it swung open. It was the orderly. "Off we go," the Navigator mumbled as he finally stirred. "Up and at 'em Air Force." It was the day after St. Patrick's Day, Saturday, March 18, 1944.

The wake up call slowly brought about two-thirds of the sleeping officers in the hut to their feet. The others, stood down on this day for various reasons, would try their best to remain in dreamland. The risers dressed for high-altitude with long johns and extra layers of warm clothing. Out to the latrine. Then he made a weak attempt at shaving only because the oxygen mask he wore grew unbelievably itchy unless he cleaned the places where it clung to his face.

The four of them set out for the briefing together: pilot Bill Sharpe from Carmel, California; Norb Bandura, copilot, from Santa Monica; bombardier Frank Richardson, Havre, Montana, and he, Bill McGuire, the navigator. He used to tease them that together with radio operator Frank Wallace from Spokane, Washington, and Ralph Huffman, flight engineer, from Atchison, Kansas, the whole front of the plane was a Wild West Show, so they had to throw him in to keep them straight. He was from Brooklyn, New York, and they called him "the old man." The Navigator had turned twenty-eight in January and if you didn't count the paddlefeet who ran the entire operation of the base, he was one of the oldest guys there. Most of the fliers were twenty-one, give or take a couple of years.

The rain and snow were lightening up and the wind had dropped to an insistent, biting hum as they joined a growing stream of bikes and foot traffic slogging their way through the mud. A good breakfast of real eggs and bacon awaited. Then it was the Operations room, and the big briefing.

To all of them, this part of England now seemed one of the sparest and most God-forsaken places on earth. It might as well have been Tasmania, or Patagonia. They say the Norfolk countryside of tiny hamlets and gently rolling farmland is lush and inviting in the kinder months of the year. Stuck in the lingering winter of 1943-1944 they couldn't imagine that.

Their base had begun operations in September and this crew came over to Station #118, as it was designated, a little later. By the time they had all gotten down to business, it seemed that there were only two kinds of weather in East Anglia: cold and damp, and cold and wet.

There were dozens and dozens of Royal Air Force and American air bases jammed into this great bulge of England that boldly juts out toward Hitler's new world order like a fist. The Navigator knew they were all just far enough apart from each other so that they could get up in the air for full scale raids without crashing together in the gray soup that on most days is morning. Barely!

Station 118, Wendling, like most of the American installations took its name from the closest railroad station. It was southeast of Kings Lynn, a good distance northeast of Cambridge and on a rough line with nearby Norwich. The base might more appropriately have been called Dereham, or even Beeston, both larger villages near at hand.

Some 300 grumpy and antsy men sat in the large room facing a small stage with a heavy curtain covering their route and destination. What the drawn curtain revealed was unusual. They were told they should be prepared for either of two missions to Germany: the first was Russleheim, near Frankfurt; the second was the same target "the old man" had been thinking about in his bunk earlier, Friedrichshafen.

Friedrichshafen was the home of the Dornier aircraft assembly plant on Lake Constance near Switzerland, where his outfit, the 392nd Bomb Group (BG) and others had been defeated by the weather on the 16th. At Friedrichshafen, the great German Zeppelins had been built and tested in the '20s and '30s. At the first sound of the name, there was a noticeable buzz in the audience of fliers. It made the Navigator uneasy. He knew it was perfectly logical to go back since they hadn't dropped a single bomb, and it was a standing policy to revisit a target as often as it took to get the job done. But it was a first for the crew of the "Sinister Minister," and on such a quick forty-eight hour turnaround, unprecedented.

They picked up some unexpected additional news at the briefing. The skies to Friedrichshafen and Augsburg on that past Thursday were not free of Goering's fighters after all. When you stretch out 600 or 800 B24s and B17s for mile after mile they don't all get to see the same war at the same time. The fliers were told that Eighth Air Force planes had brought down seventy-five German fighters while all the 392nd saw were clouds and flak.

Scuttlebutt also had it that other units had lost heavy bombers that day, particularly among the B17s. No cakewalk after all.

The general briefing ran almost ninety minutes and then pilots, and copilots, bombardiers and navigators split off for specialized meetings on the two possible missions. "The old man" signed the roll sheet releasing the navigator's sealed flight folder, which provided him with the check points he needed to match their progress to the target and back. At the equipment room they checked personal belongings and donned their electrically heated flying suits and fleece-lined leather outerwear, drawing whatever added gear they required.

The Eighth Air Force's daylight precision bombing raids hinged on tight formation flying as their primary defense. The planes largely played follow the leader, but the navigator's job was to know his plane's true position at all times. Only Bill McGuire's calculations would keep "Sinister Minister" exactly where it needed to be, round trip. If any of the Eighth's bombers had to break formation or were separated for any reason, the navigator would set the course home or to an alternative. For many, Switzerland became the next best choice after England. But it depended on geography, the pilot's rapid judgment, and many factors outside their control. On the American heavy bombers, each crewman had multiple functions and assignments. Bill's back up job was to take over the nose turret guns, if the need arose, whenever the bombardier was otherwise occupied or unable. The navigator was also expected to make a record of any information about downed and damaged planes in the group as spotted by him or reported by the crew on the interphone.

Bill stood waiting for mass with a large group of combat crew members when he learned it was official. Forget about Frankfurt. They were once again going to Friedrichshafen. Then they heard that the religious service was canceled. Father Paul McDonough, God bless him, had overslept!

Lieutenant McGuire was the last man out to the hardstand to board "Sinister Minister." He took one last loop around the ship before going to the hatch. Now in the distance he saw Chaplain McDonough racing between B24s in a jeep. The priest offered quick communion and last minute blessings wherever he stopped.

Their "J" was one of the few in the group and they'd only had it a short time. Most of the 392nd flew the "H" model. The differences weren't that obvious and weren't all positive. The J featured a hydraulically operated nose turret and a simplified fuel transfer system. It had a noticeably different top turret than the H. And the nosewheel door opened inwardly instead of outwardly, which confused everybody. The J was heavier, sturdier but as a result a little more sluggish to handle according to Billy Sharpe and his copilot, Bandura. Both planes had heavy, retractable ball turrets. In B24s, bombardier and navigator were squashed into the nose, forward and below the cockpit. In both the H and the J, improved defensive measures for the nose turret only cramped things further for the occupants. More importantly, they restricted forward visibility in the nose. Command was aware of the ship's limitations but, for the time being, nothing could be done about it. The task at hand was winning the war.

Lieutenant McGuire felt his feet leave the ground as he swung up into the J through the main hatch. He deliberately entered through the back of the plane so he could see the rest of the crew before climbing into the nose. Nate Maylander, tailgunner and armorer, had been hard at work since the briefing with cleaning and checking their weapons and setting up their ammo supply. He had a heavy belt of alternating fifty caliber slugs around his neck. He gave the Navigator the OK sign as Bill moved through the waist. Nathan brought a little more Brooklyn, New York to #117. He hailed from a section near Coney Island. Waist gunners Mike Cugini and Carl Anderson, respectively of Buffalo, New York and Perry, Iowa, gave him honest smiles and thumbs up. Standing just forward of them, though, was a strange face. Anderson introduced Bill to Clarence Covenez, Crooked Creek, Pennsylvania, who explained that he was subbing in the ball turret. The Navigator asked what had happened to McGowan, their usually dependable belly gunner. Cugini shrugged: "Nobody knows, Lieutenant."

The Navigator made his way across the bomb bay catwalk connecting the two parts of the plane and squeezed down into the nose, nodding to Richardson, the bombardier.

He quickly laid out and arranged his instruments, maps, and equipment on the small table space he had. Then he checked in with the cockpit on the interphone. "Good morning, Lieutenant McGuire," Sharpe bellowed. "You know we wouldn't leave without you, and, as I was just explaining to my worthy copilot here, it is understandable that a man of your advanced years might move a little slower than most." "Albeit, mein pilot," answered the Navigator, "let's just see how quickly you two can finish the checklist and get this overloaded crate off the ground."

As he began to work on some preliminary figures, Bill heard the familiar voices of radio operator Frank Wallace and flight engineer Ralph Huffman. Wallace sat behind the copilot, in a little compartment with his equipment, facing the right wing and engines three and four. The flight engineer also manned the top turret above and behind the cockpit. Other than the officers, he had seniority over the crew and was responsible for monitoring engine performance and fuel consumption.

Lieutenant McGuire continued making rapid calculations at his table, which faced aft and was just above the nose wheel hatch. Through his small window, he could see engines one and two. He could also see the shifting feet of pilot Sharpe and copilot Bandura through a gap in the cockpit control wall. Similarly, they could turn aft and see the dangling feet of Huffman hanging down from his top turret perch.

As he worked through the math, the Navigator didn't hear the bombardier as much as he could smell him. He realized that he couldn't have smelled much better himself. Was it just the heavy fleece-lined leather suits at ground level and the activity, he wondered? Or was it closer to the ancient perfume of fear? But bombardiers always seemed to be burly guys, he told himself. All very cozy in any event. Snug as a bug in a rug, as his sweet bride would have put it!

The Navigator saw the engines fire and catch one at a time and "Sinister Minister" began to taxi. He never took well to the fumes and, at this point, was always a little jumpy. He had this weird, almost wistful urge to be somewhere else, anywhere else. But was glad, as always, to at last be underway.

Coming on the news of this abrupt return to Friedrichshafen, Billy McGowan was the second thing to go wrong, he thought. The Dead End Kid, they called him. He had been with them since the start. Gangling, slightly goofy in appearance, with a sleepy grin and an off-centered baseball cap on his head, he kept everybody in good spirits. And no one could get to him. He was their unanimous lucky mascot; but not today. What had happened? Maybe just filling in for someone else on another ship. That's the way it went sometimes. Musical chairs. Thinking of McGowan for some reason made "the old man" think of his own son. His birthday was in two weeks, he remembered, and it would be his first. The Navigator resolved to get him some little thing quick and send it off to the States. At least a card. Mick would like that, he mused, with the mental picture of his twenty-year-old wife before him. It wouldn't get there in time, but at least she would know that he had remembered.

He and Frank Richardson moved into their takeoff positions. All four engines roared at full throttle as they started down the mile and a bit that it would take to lift a full load of bombs and fuel off the main runway, over the tree line and straight up. As they gathered more speed, only scattered clouds flew above them. The Navigator saw that it would be a beautiful day. It was just after 0940 hours and the "Sinister Minister" was airborne.

The Navigator's son was born on April Fool's Day, 1943 at Norwegian Hospital in Brooklyn. From the first, I was brought up to respect my father's name -- it was also my own --and his memory, of which I had none of my own. My mother, Muriel, and I lived in her parents' house. I did visit my other grandparents who lived nearby, but not too often. There were strains and differences it seemed, but most of all I had an early sense that I was a kind of bridge between the two families. And, in that same formal context, I was also a material symbol of their pain and their loss. A child dramatizes, particularly to enhance his or her self-importance. But the weight of the family tragedy, my father's death, was fresh and real. It hung on me like oversized winter clothing. Gradually, I learned that no one could be blamed for the situation, and that growing awareness made me quietly angry. My mother moved willfully and aggressively to get past the mourning and all the looking back on the past. In some ways, this only added to the misunderstanding, the hurt, and the sense of guilt that surrounded us all.

There were cousins around the busy household but I was also very much an only child, a solitary child in a world largely made up of adults. And in this world I held a special status that no one ever spoke of. I was "The Boy." It was a loaded phrase full of irony, loss, and hope.

In my grandmother's house, behind the kitchen, there was a narrow room used as a walk-in closet. Here is where I first encountered my father directly, because hanging there were the Navigator's uniforms, and other contents of his footlocker returned to the widow as next of kin. I felt the rough woolen material, smelled the leather, and gazed at the shiny Air Force buttons. I longed to reach the campaign hat with its eagle insignia high up on the shelf above. Much later it would be within reach.

My dad was a local hero in more ways than one. He had been a pretty good all-around athlete as a schoolboy and went on to captain the Brooklyn College Kingsmen varsity basketball team in the late 1930s. And he was active as a volunteer coach for youngsters. The neighborhood where my parents' families lived was in the Sunset Park section of South Brooklyn, near the singularly unlovely Gowanus Expressway, at the northern border of Bay Ridge. Bay Ridge, and its gracious Shore Road, stand along the Narrows between Brooklyn and Staten Island at the entrance to New York Harbor. The neighborhood between Bay Ridge and Sunset Park was dominated by a city block-long Roman Catholic church, school, and residential complex high on a hill. This was an era when residents of the boroughs were identified by their parish church, and theirs was Our Lady of Perpetual Help. OLPH was like a fortress, with great granite walls looming above everything.

After college the Navigator continued to play basketball for the parish in the CYO or Catholic Youth Organization men's program. Home games were widely attended events then, with a dance following the final horn. After the war, the parish established various trophies to honor both the late Second Lieutenant Bill McGuire, and a teammate of his, Jack Hallisey, another airman killed in the European theater.

In the late 1940s, the same building that had served as the gym and a men's club was pressed into service as a kindergarten by the parish. And here was where I first went to school and was publicly bade to observe the trophy case with its gold icons and photographs of the two war heroes by the black-habited teacher. When the kindergarten class was instructed by the Sister in charge on how to shoot a basketball properly, I was the first to volunteer and promptly and mightily threw the ball back over my head in the wrong direction – sending my classmates into convulsions of noisy derision, much to the consternation of the nun.

The boy did not do well in school. I was slow, lanky, and self-absorbed, almost melancholy. The classes, pulsing with the early signs of a budding baby boom, were quite large. I was lost by the first grade. One day I was mysteriously pulled out of class and led through the cool marble halls to the principal's office. The Sister told me I had a visitor, as she took me past the framed Madonna and Child outside her office to a small meeting room. "This is a man who flew with your dad in the war," she said. "He wants to talk with you."

We sat on opposite ends of a heavy, polished pine table under a crucifix on the wall. The principal left us alone in the semi-dark room and closed the door behind her. I saw a gaunt, nervous-looking young man who looked back at me curiously. The man seemed perched on the chair like a perilously piled stack of blocks rather than truly sitting in it. He began, almost as if he were talking to someone else, behind me: "Yes. I knew your dad, over there. And we flew together. In the bombers. You know about that. And, you are his son." I nodded my head to this. Our eyes met. There was a long silence and the young man seemed to be struggling… for words. He stared at my child's pale face and blood bright tie and then his red eyes began to water. "He was just such a great guy," his voice caught and he suddenly sobbed. And then, he began to cry. "Your dad, never forget, he was a hero." His body shook with sobs, and his head drooped down toward the table. He could continue no more.

I watched the flier cry for several moments and then got down out of the chair, opened the door, and went to get the nuns to help the man.

My mom was furious when she heard about this episode and threatened to sue the school should anything like that happen again. I never saw or heard from the airman after that. I never learned his name.

The house where we lived, a parlor-floor and basement row house, stood directly across the street from the OLPH church and rectory. I could stand in a second floor bedroom bay window or under the ledge of the red sandstone stoop in the airyway entrance and watch the uncertain moods of the basilica shift with the changing light and weather. It was a kind of mysterious castle in my young mind. In the rain, I saw rivulets turn into roaring streams as they cascaded down the tiered copper roofs and drain spouts. And always, I watched the faithful come and go.

The church school had a marching band, fife and drum corps, and a large military drill unit. "The cadets," we all called them, for their West Point-style uniforms. And every parade filed past my window. In the years after the war, however, too many of the parades were somber marches: an armed services contingent, dipped colors, an open hearse, and a flag-draped coffin. The last fighting men were coming home past my window. But young as I was, I was made to understand that the Navigator would not be coming back. My mother was certain, despite official assurances, that any attempt to ship him back would result in burying some other body in his name. She would have no part of it. I wondered about these things with wide eyes as the funeral corteges wound up the Brooklyn street to the muffled staccato of the cadet drums.

In the hospital, while I was just recovering from a tonsillectomy, I saw another patient, a dark-haired man, wheeled by on a gurney. Something in my expression caught his eye and the man gave me a warm smile. As the effects of the anesthetic wore off only slowly, I thought, "Maybe that's him. Maybe he's back and it was all just a big mix-up."

I was devoted to my mother. One on one we were a certain thing. Pals. We could make each other laugh, and she would always love children madly. She called me Magillicuddy, Magee, Magoo, Ishkabibble and Schnooks. While our circumstances were not unique, there is still something both comical and poignant about a little shaver, such as I was, feeling knowing and protective of a grown woman, like she was my kid sister, but I did. I was proud of her beauty, her goodness, even her flashes of anger, because she had character and heart.

But she had never had time to finish her character and to fully mature when I came, the death came, and tremendous pressures built up around her. She trusted her instinct but she was also a mass of insecurity. She worried about what people would think when there was hardly any cause for concern. She fretted over people's motivations and read telltale signs of human behavior like a deck of tarot cards. I loved her dearly but we both sensed we were in a kind of trap.

My mother, nicknamed Micky or Mick, was the youngest of six surviving children. She was just nineteen when I was born. She worked for the phone company and then for a big liquor distributor in Manhattan. She was deeply hurt and troubled after my dad was reported missing. It wasn't until the summer of '46 that his death was confirmed. Her father died shortly thereafter. She was very attached to him. She liked to party more and more, to take risks, to leave herself vulnerable to more hurt. And it came. It always made me feel sad that I somehow couldn't make her happy.

In late 1949, she married Al Raggio, one of the liquor salesmen at work, and I was sent to a Catholic boarding school in Manhattan, St. Ann's Academy for Boys. They lived in various apartments in Greenwich Village, on West 11th St., 95 Christopher St., West 16th St. and finally, Stuyvesant Town, on the east side of 14th St. She continued to work.

I joined them on weekends, holidays, and vacations. At night, in school, during the first years, I couldn't help feeling a little abandoned. After lights out, I romanticized about finding love that would accept me just as I was. Unconditional love, which I imagined was not only the right kind but the only kind.

My stepfather came from a large first generation Italian-American family raised in New York's Greenwich Village. He was devoted to his sisters and brother and spoke of his mother as if she were a saint. But nothing was ever said about his father. I came to believe over time that this absence made it that much harder for him to be a father to me. Although considerably older than my mother, my new dad, like my mom, was a product of the Depression. His family had survived through a no-nonsense pragmatism and a hard-bitten peasant mentality that left a permanent mark on him. He was a you-give-something-you-get-something kind of guy. Life was a series of transactions. Anything else was so much hooey. He also had charm, a sense of humor of sorts; he was very much a man of the streets, a New York character. But he didn't believe in much more than himself and the art of survival. My mother and Al were not a match made in heaven. They were however, more or less loyal to the bitter end. Opposites attract. Underneath the friction and the furious struggles they cared for each other. But it was never enough. And, like so many youngsters in similar situations, I was right in the middle.

For some reason, the Archdiocese was pushing down the age for Confirmation to under ten years at this time, at least for my school. During preparations for this ceremony my mother explained to me that my stepfather wanted to adopt me, to officially make me his son. But it was up to me, she said, and we talked about how it would change my last name.

It didn't take me very long to come to a conclusion. I said I didn't see how I could do that because I was my father's son and I already had his name. Mother said not to worry about it, but it came up again, a few more times. The boy always arrived at the same conclusion.

I got to spend a lot of my free time at my Grandma's house in Brooklyn and with my playmates from the street across from OLPH. My "Gram" was named Julia, nee Cople; she was born in Brooklyn in 1888 and married Peter McLaughlin as a young woman. Mr. Cople, her grandfather, according to legend, ran away from a Prussian military school as a teenager and managed to get on a steamer to New York. So, while I was mostly Irish-American in heritage, there was a sliver of Deutschland in my genealogy.

Julia was short, round, compact and full of life and surprises. Her bright dark eyes were framed in wire spectacles and her head was capped in a helmet of thinning gray ringlets, cut close and curled like the ends of ribbons on a birthday gift. She drank, she swore, she played the horses. She expressed herself plainly; you had no doubt where she stood and her affection for me was as sure and honest as her bone-crushing embrace.

And in my childhood, particularly the early years, it was my grandmother who came to my emotional rescue. Gram, who made cream puffs, delicious vegetable soups and stews for me, and who told me that it would all be all right, a promise and a prophecy. Gram, who would play games with me on a dare and prove despite her girth how spry she was by touching her toes or suddenly giving me chase. Gram, who would take me on mysterious neighborhood treks to meet the man with the clipboard in storefronts or in parked cars, men who I much later realized were bookmakers. Gram, who, much to my wonder and revulsion, might fry herself up an eel for breakfast as was her father's habit before her. Gram, who planted a large box turtle in the backyard for me to find as a magically reincarnated replacement for the tiny one I had buried, with tears in my eyes, the year before. Gram, who would speak to her grown sons and her peers about my mother's woes only in "pig Latin" so as not to "let on to the boy." She, who would talk to herself intently while primping in the living room mirror for some important appearance, until my mimicking faces behind her broke the spell of her soliloquy. She, who would regale me with stories of her own turn-of-the-century Brooklyn childhood, like walking out on the partially frozen waters of New York Bay, or sitting on the lap of Buffalo Bill in her grandmother's waterfront saloon.

And when I was tall and feisty, Gram could still confront my playful smile with a scowl and, with fists dug into her hips, would say: "A wise guy Charlie, hey. I'll give you one swift kick in the behind if you don't watch out. Think I can't reach that high," she'd warn. "Well, we'll see, we'll see."

My memories of her husband, Pete, my grandpa, are spare and hazy. I remember his stature, his towering over me, although he was not a tall man. He was broad in the chest and carried himself like a big man. I remember lying on top of his prone frame with the newspaper spread out before us both so he could read me the Sunday funnies. Vaguely, I remember the ambulance gurney that took him away when he died, but older cousins insist that I was too young. He had had stomach problems and died of internal complications. Alcohol played a role.

But his spirit was always alive in that Brooklyn household. His portrait sat high in the dining room where his brood inevitably gathered for holidays and special occasions. He was remembered, memorialized, with respect and affection. And Julia, despite the big family around her, missed him sorely to the end. Now, those of us who remain and remember miss her sorely too. For she always had a way of holding you, and she still does. Pete and Julia are one with life, love and laughter. But most of all, they gave each of their own a sense of family and it lives on.

In the summer, when I was a boy, my mom and stepdad would often rent a place at some local vacation spot for a month or two. Twice, they sent me away to a camp in New Hampshire. When the parents returned to work, Julia was my overseer at places like Cedarwood Park, New Jersey, Sag Harbor, Long Island and Lake Valhalla, near Fishkill and Cold Spring in the Hudson Valley of New York.

Gram was of the old school. She would go around turning out electric lights, unless they were truly needed. "Place is all lit up like Luna Park," she would grumble. So on one late August evening after supper, alone in the house in Lake Valhalla, we sat in the living room as darkness and the night sounds closed in all around us. I was in a wingback armchair, unusually still and quiet. She, who taught herself to play by ear, sat at the piano and made simple music with the last rays of the sun the only light.

"Gramma," I spoke, "are the Germans bad people?" "No, son," she said, continuing to play. "They're the same as everyone else, good eggs and bad, just like everyone else… but the Nazis, they're sons of bitches." It was said as much to herself as to me. "Good eggs and bad," she repeated, her voice tailing off. Only the piano then. "Your father," she said, after a while, the final glint of daylight reflected in her glasses, "he was one of the good ones."

Despite the burden of a full load of fuel and **bombs**, the "Sinister Minister," climbing at over 150 feet per minute, soon reached assembly altitude and formed up with the group. Bill McGuire's squadron, the 579th, was flying lead today, with Major Myron Keilman in the copilot's seat of Captain Vern Baumgart's "El Lobo." While normally the soup demanded a nail-biting spiral ascent around the radio beacon, today was relatively straightforward. CAVU, ceiling and visibility unlimited weather, made all the difference. Pilot Bill Sharpe tucked in directly behind Lieutenant Books, Baumgart's left wing, and they all slowly circled, taking on the rest of the twenty-eight planes the 392nd sent up.

In the waist, Mike Cugini pivoted his gun and looked out past King's Lynn to the sea. He felt good about this one, that it would bring him closer to home. He dreamed of sailing back into New York Harbor with all the guys and taking the train, no, flying up to Buffalo to be together once again with his Arlene, and all the people he loved. These guys, he loved them too. There was no other word for it.

Mike remembered their last base in the States together. Salina, and toward the end, Topeka, Kansas - and the hottest August and September on record. The air corps played it by the book: officers and "enlisted" men. But they all stuck together as much as they could. There was nothing phony about it. They were a crew, a unit, a team. There was nothing to drink in that dry county but "near beer." They had had their fill of that swill and as the endless days burned on and the pressure of an uncertain embarkation grew, they all decided it was time for a break. And they all -- more or less, kind of, with thin cover stories -- went over the hill. Briefly. For a weekend in Kansas City, where a man could get a drink.

They didn't worry so much about the consequences. The old man said it was all right. The old man had always gotten them home and did whatever fixin' their adventures required. The old man would get them back again. They were in all kinds of bars, classy and not-so-classy, and everybody was buying and everybody wanted to tell them that they'd be okay and they'd win the war.

They crashed in one hotel room. They had pushed two beds together and six of them fell across them. One on an easy chair, one on a love seat. Somebody was on the floor. Two days and nights like that. But then the dawn came and somehow they all knew, staring into each other's hairy faces and bloodshot eyes, that something was wrong, very wrong.

Back in Topeka they learned what it was. Their Replacement Training Unit of substitute crews was gone, planes and personnel. Headed east for England it seemed and a date with Herr Hitler. They were all summarily chewed out and made to sweat it out. But in the end they got what they thought they'd get. They were put on a slow train to New York to catch a boat to meet up with their group for that date with Herr Hitler. So the party continued en route, more card games, more drinks, and no more guilt. In the big city, with twenty-four hours leave, Mike had taken the subway to Grand Central Station to catch a train to see his girl. It was a quick visit but great. He slept on the train back and took a cab to the assembly point. Just under the wire. The guys all razzed him. But not the old man. He just smiled, shook his hand and said, "I knew you'd make it."

In the nose of "Sinister Minister," the Navigator noted the flares of recognition as they swung in after the 44th Bomb Group and proceeded for the coast and rendezvous with the rest of the Eighth's strike force. "Behind the Eight Balls again," shouted Richardson from his forward position. The 44th for whatever reasons, warranted or not, was known as a hard luck group and they chose the hapless nickname "The Flying Eight Balls" as an intended gesture of defiance. Together with the 392nd they formed the Second Division's 14th Combat Wing.

Returning his gaze to the figures in front of him, Lt. McGuire made one more note and then set down his E6B computer, a kind of circular slide rule developed for aerial navigation. Resting on his elbows, he cupped his head in his hands and closed his eyes for just a moment. ETA with the other 600 plus planes, not counting the fighter support, would be in about six minutes. Assuming everyone made the linkup on time, then the big parade would begin its long run across the Channel, France and Germany. What did Maylander say? What did he call it? "Ah, yes," he told himself, "like Steeplechase. A long bumpy ride over obstacles. You hang on for dear life and you can't get off till its over. And then somebody yells, hey, let's go on again."

Looking out the nose past Richardson, Bill could see the rest of the section, with Everhart on the Major's right wing and Spartage covering his tail to Books' right. He knew Tausley, the Spartage navigator. Behind the 579th were eight planes of the 578th in two groups of four, behind, above, and below the six in the lead. Behind them a similar group of fourteen representing the 576th and 577th squadrons. "There they are," Richardson said. More flares and a whole lot of B17s and B24s. Assembly for the main force.

In the high group, to the right of the "Sinister Minister," Lt. Cliff Peterson in "Big Time Operator,"#981, realized his copilot had been quiet much too long. "What's on your mind, Russ," he asked turning to him. Russ Vreiling smiled back at him and patted his holster: "Just thinkin' if all else fails I'll get some good pops in with my old 45." They laughed, but Peterson knew that Russ meant it because on the Gotha raid in February, he had seen the copilot slide open his window and start shooting at the German fighters as they passed. Peterson had had to order Vreiling back to the controls.

The pilot asked his engineer for a fuel consumption check. Hugh Hinshaw gave him the reading and then went 360 degrees in the top turret to survey the long lines of heavies making their way southeast now, out over the Channel and away from England.

Hinshaw knew how to use his twin guns, 20 percent of the firepower #981 had, from the position of advantage he had above the rest of the plane. He heard the voice of the bombardier, Ed Brown, on the intercom and gritted his teeth. Hugh Malcolm Hinshaw, a West Virginia hillbilly to most of the airmen who didn't know much else about him, knew a thing or two about men and leadership. "Pete" Peterson was a man Hinshaw would follow gladly and give a thousand percent for. On the other hand, he wouldn't give two cents for Ed Brown. He was nothing but an arrogant pain to Hinshaw. The engineer had seen the officer demonstrate it time and time again. They all sized Brown up the same way. Hinshaw looked forward to being able to test his guns out over the Channel when "Pete" gave the OK, so he could blow off some of the steam he generated just hearing the bombardier's voice.

The long line of planes stretched for several miles, gradually gaining more altitude now. In addition to Friedrichshafen, the task force would later split to hit the Munich region and two more targets: Oberpfaffenhofen and Augsburg. In advance of the 14th Combat Wing, and to its left, was a force of B17s and among them, the 390th Bomb Group.

Aboard the 390th's "Rosie," #925, pilot Robert "Wade" Biesecker remembered Augsburg as he reminded the Fortress crew to plug in at 11,000 feet altitude. He checked all six lines that covered oxygen, heat for the body suit and communications and pulled down his goggles. It always made him feel a little silly, like a "Buck Rogers" comic strip. But in an unpressurized, increasingly frozen atmosphere, it was vital to their ability to function and survive. The 390th had been to Augsburg on the 16th and pounded the crap out of them, he thought. Now, it was deja vu. They continued to climb. Encountered some cloudiness for the first time -- but plowed on through it with their four 1,200 horsepower engines pushing them on.

In the radio compartment, another West Virginian, Harry Houck felt the cold steel of his gun grips through two pairs of gloves. The slip stream blowing into the open portal felt like a headache on his face. A familiar headache. But he laughed into the wind. This was number twenty-three. Even with the new tour combat missions requirements, Harry was almost home.

The "Sinister Minister" was turning as it continued to ascend. The Navigator knew Lt. Sharpe was following the command of the lead and they in turn were following the 44th BG. "But what the hell are they doing," McGuire asked aloud? He realized that he had said it over the interphone but the pilot had no reproof for him; Sharpe was asking himself the same question.

Behind "Sinister Minister" in the 578th's lead low position, aboard pilot Rex Johnson's #465, another navigator was also puzzling over this slowly continuing turn. Delmar Johnson had figured that the group was already running behind schedule. Now Del realized that the 44th, on encountering some light, unforecast cloud cover in the distance, had chosen not to approach the French coast directly. Although it looked like they could soon be in the clear anyway, the 44th was making a 360 degree climbing turn or complete circle to get above the same thin clouds.

When they had straightened out once again, Del checked his watch and his calculations and warned pilot Johnson that they were now running close to twenty minutes behind their original IP schedule, the initial point for the start of the bomb run. What he didn't say was what they were all thinking. This was pushing it for their fighters which would, in all likelihood, be leaving the rendezvous over target before the 392nd got to Friedrichshafen. The fighters didn't have the fuel capacity to simply sit and wait.

Back on the "Sinister Minister," almost to a man, the crew had quickly come to the same inescapable conclusion. "The old man" was reminded of basketball. What a team sport it was. And how, when he had played well and lost, it didn't matter that he had played well. Coming off the St. Francis game in the Garden in front of 17,000 fans in '38, he had had one of his best games ever, after a knee injury earlier in the season. Everything clicked for him in this come from behind victory. But then they faced Clair Bee's L.I.U. team, one of the best in the country. Bill was making the same moves and it felt good, but everything was going the wrong way for the rest of them. Long Island threw Brooklyn off its game and the Kingsmen couldn't get it back. Whatever he did right, L.I.U. did twice as much and the score mounted. They got disheartened. They got killed. The Kingsmen fell a long way down.

Now, however, he resolved to get it out of his mind. The player, he told himself, always plays through. He just plays through. No matter what, you did your job. That was part of teamwork too.

Some of the 392nd planes were experiencing mechanical difficulties and beginning to lag or come away from their formations. The group was at 19,000 feet and climbing as it crossed the French coast at 1230 hours. In #174, in the last position in the second contingent, the pilot, Lt. Gerald Dalton, responded to a general order to tighten up but then drifted too close to the propeller wash of Lt. John Feran's #651.

Aboard #371, "The Doodle Bug," waist gunner John Bode saw through binoculars as Dalton fought but lost. Dalton's #174 wallowed and slid with magnetic force into the tail of Feran's Liberator. It severed the tail and tail assembly. Both ships began to break up and fall. Then they collided a second time and exploded in sheets of flame, crashing down near Amiens. One chute was recorded by the spotters. Only one.

It took some time for the word to be communicated to the lead group. But Maylander in the tail of #117 had reported seeing the explosion in the distance. The Wendling group's total force was suddenly reduced by six Liberators. Four of the B24s had aborted at the coast because of various unrelated mechanical problems. The 392nd was lagging behind now, trying to fill slots, tighten up, and then pick up some time. In the "Sinister Minister," the Navigator noted the collision along with the fact that it was the third thing that had gone wrong.

There is a school of thought among the children of those killed in the war that people, society, the great unwashed American public, does not want to hear from us. In fact, people would like us to be invisible as well as silent. To just go away. This isn't a whine, it is an observation. Personally, I've never given much credence to such thinking, but I can attest that growing up with a shadowy hero father can leave one with certain quirks.

As a boy I learned to be quiet and passive, to go along with things. This can become a useful strategy and a creative force. Unfortunately, it can also build some resentment. It is possible to turn this kind of background into a well-developed critical and analytical faculty, and that was my path out of myself, along with some gift for language and expression. And although I was, I suppose, an affectionate child and always very much in tune with my own feelings, I noticed while growing up that I wasn't a particularly empathic person. That was something I had to work at and grow into. Still do. Of course, in my case there wasn't any natural progression of nurturing and positive self-image building.

34

It was much more of a catch as catch can development. So I grew up, in jolts and spurts, but always looking for approval. We, the WWII fatherless, do that a lot.

The boy grew tall, went to high school and college. I married Bernadette, the sweetheart of my teen years, and we had two sons and later, two daughters. I became a public relations director in the broadcasting business in New York City and still later, in the insurance industry. We bought a house in a tree-lined suburb on Long Island Sound. I was a commuter.

Through it all, questions from my earliest days nagged at my consciousness. I had been brought up on the mantra that my dad was a hero, a brave flier who died for his country. But the details were vague. What exactly had happened to the first Bill McGuire and what happened to his bomber crew mates?

I poured myself into my family. Making up for something that had been missing in my earlier life, I realized that I was a bit obsessive about it. We were a tightly-knit bunch, the six of us, but I wasn't always the most patient parent or the most realistic. I wasn't the best provider either. There were authority figure conflicts, and that ever popular struggle between personal goals and hopes and the demands of the work situation. I tended to internalize the things I couldn't successfully balance in my life. But I always saw myself as a player and the game wasn't over till it was over. Helping each other, we braved out the rough spots and grew stronger as a family.

So life went on, but the questions about 1944 were always there on my mind. What had happened, I asked myself? I had the right, I felt, to know as much as anyone knew. But how to get at it? How to go about it? Most of all, if possible, I thought I was after some assurance that my dad was at peace.

As if it wasn't enough to be secretly plagued by these questions, the culture after the war bombarded me with it as I grew.

In boarding school, explaining to other kids why my last name wasn't the same as my mother's. "You don't even have a father," was always a great taunt in a spat. On "movie nights," seeing *Command Decision* and *Twelve O'clock High.* Studying WWII in class. Armed Forces Day and the drone of bombers parading over the city. Memorial Day: "A poppy for your lapel?" In a thousand ways, some subtle, some direct, personal, confrontational, it was there. It was always there. What happened to him?

In the 70s I made my first official inquiries to the Air Force. I was told that as a result of a major fire at the St. Louis records center they had lost the service record and data that corresponded to my father.

My mother passed away in the second week of November in 1976. She died of kidney and liver damage brought on by alcoholism. She had just turned fifty-three on the 6th. Grandma Julia died a few days before her. My mother had never really deserted me. She was full of a fierce pride and love for me and my young family. She simply had never been strong enough to get past the hurt of 1944. To me, in a very real sense, she had been shot down too.

My picture of Micky, my mom, is colored with guilt. Emotionally, through the years of my youth, I was running from her tortured misery, while she in her own way, tough on the outside, soft and uncertain underneath, was crying out for help, for rescue. At times I used my hard won identity as a young family man as a cover to safely distance myself. To if not sever, then at least to deaden the psychological connection. I was there for her on the surface, with all the obligatory appearances, but I wasn't sound enough, mature enough, in my twenties and early thirties, to take matters in hand. I walked a fine line. When I went over that line I could literally make myself sick with concern and frustration. Any exchange with her could, if I let it, very quickly become about me, rather than her, and simultaneously I would be both back in her grip again and powerless to help her. Mother's disease, however, made no allowances. It took no prisoners. It was total, and I will never know with certainty if I could have made a difference.

At the start, Micky and Al, my stepfather, had a lot going for them. They were a good looking couple with a comfortable life, a summer home, books, clothes, jewelry, vacations, a wide circle of friends, and nearby family to lend added support. But it all fell apart rapidly and the seeds of that broken promise were sewn in patterns of neglect and abuse from the beginning.

The prewar Sunset Park, Brooklyn neighborhood was solidly working class but for a long, long time there wasn't much work, even in the nearby docks and Bush Terminal industrial complex. The Great Depression. Once, years later, when she was drunk, my mother told me about getting a bicycle as a child for her birthday. It was the one true gift of her dreams, she said. It was no beat up hand-me-down passed along from her older brothers and sister, but something new, bright, and perfect and just for her. Proof that she too, was special to her mom and dad. But my grandparents couldn't keep up the payments, so they had to take it from her and return it. There she was, a mature woman, telling me, her twenty-year-old son about this incident as if it was still a fresh little girl hurt, a momentous event.

Sunset Park however, was a neighborhood, a post-prohibition culture, that always had a few dollars for drink. On the avenue, Fifth Avenue, along the shopping strips, you literally could not walk a block on either side of the street without finding one or more saloons or beer gardens. To many, beer was mother's milk, and on Sundays after church, the baby carriages would park in front of the bars for family conviviality. Drinking was part of ceremonies both large and small. The *alpha* and *omega*. Life was a rusty door but alcohol oiled the hinges.

The rumblings of war in the late 1930s brought comparative good times to the old neighborhood as Brooklyn and America bustled, turning out and shipping out, all the stuff the world needed to stock up on for the coming killing frenzy. It was get it while you can time. The drinking, the party, got noisier, rowdier, more intense.

Micky, while hardly more than a child, was at the party too. The runt of the litter, she couldn't help but notice how a couple of drinks loosened her wit and her already sharp tongue. Made her feel more at ease. She could keep up with the others, her older peers and give as good as she got. She could fit in. They all laughed at her jokes, laughed with her, not at her. They all loved Micky and it was a comfortable feeling, like family card games in the kitchen. Like home. But it was richer than innocence. It had an edge. There was power there too. Her power. She felt it.

My mother married my father when she was eighteen, full of youthful optimism and ambition, though the war clouds were closing in and he wore an Army uniform. She bet that it could not, would not happen to him. That was his bet too. She was in love with an older man, a handsome man, and only good things would come of it. She felt beautiful, even glamorous. As good as anybody on the planet.

At twenty, she was a widow with a child. A child with his eyes. Then the war was over and everybody was dancing in the streets, dancing with glee. But it was a hollow victory for her. It was the biggest party yet, but she felt that she didn't belong. Her brothers came home from the war to their families. Life rushed on, closing in around her, but everything was strange. Alternately, there was crushing pain and numbness. No one could help her. No one could understand. She was scared and part of her, she realized, was already dead.

Gradually, she came around, to me, the boy, and to the concerns of others. To work, to friendship, to laughter, even to possibility. And to the men, who made her notice their noticing her. She looked in the mirror and saw a harder face under the make up and she resolved to be hard, to move on. To give as good as she got.

At the liquor company where she worked, Heublein's, there was a little bar in the office reception area. Some time after 5 p.m., work would shut down and the party would resume. Micky was making them laugh again. She fit in just fine. But it no longer felt safe. It no longer felt like home. It just pushed these things away, far away, as if they didn't matter. As if she didn't care. And there were times when she thought it might be possible to stop caring. To just forget. For if she could stop remembering, the pain might be gone, and she could at last let go. Just let go.

She began a spiraling behavior where heavy drinking led to more and more absences from work. At first it was hardly noticeable to anyone but family and a few close friends. Over the years, it became a bigger and bigger problem, obvious to all but a few. When I was very young, I might find her in bed in the late morning or early afternoon, sick, downhearted, tormented. Those things I could sense. I didn't know, however, what hungover meant. No, mommy was very sick, and she said I made it worse by not doing well in school. I had to do better. I had to do what she said or she might not get better.

Postwar America was for starting over. That was what it was all about. Bargains and opportunities abounded. You didn't look back, you moved on, and in this, at least, Micky was right in step. She was determined to pull herself out of her misery and to make a new start for the two of us. It was her only real option and she would give it her best shot.

My stepdad, Al, worked in taverns and restaurants in New York before the war. He was tough and street smart. He took it all in, how it all worked. He learned how the restaurant kitchens worked too. By the time he was drafted into the Army, he had become a cook. They stuck him in a prisoner of war camp in Texas, but he didn't prepare meals for the Germans, only for his American officers. Made sergeant that way. After the war, his contacts in the old Greenwich Village neighborhood and the restaurant trade led him to the companies that supplied booze and wine to the local package shops and dining joints. He was a commission man, and that part of it was close to his soul. He was no nine-to- fiver but, as a salesman, a man who could control his own fate. If he ever needed more money at any given time, he could go out and find a way to make it, while salaried people just sat on their behinds and whined.

Al saw enough bias in his life to teach me to be unbiased. He had so little education in his life that he encouraged my full education. He loved to entertain, to cook a meal for guests and to present it with every detail perfected. "Food should please the eye as well as the taste," he taught me, and every meal was a celebration of life. Yet, he was suspicious of those who shared his meals, suspicious that they might abuse his generosity. He taught me many things, but nothing about the presence of love. He was always afraid of love, that it might exist. That he might be missing it. But he could not move toward it. This was his only real bias, and like all prejudice, it twisted him.

Micky and Al found each other at the party, and in the true postwar spirit began anew, a married couple in the eyes of God and man. "Always" was their wedding song. Soon they were arguing. It quickly got physical, on both sides. My mother still gave as good as she got. They had, in the end, few things in common but they both liked to drink. And I was the little peacemaker, the intermediary, the messenger for their war games. It was an indelible experience that left me with a visceral distaste for conflict and a sense of embarrassed unease about personal confrontation and dispute that persists to this day.

Much of this was held in check until my college years. Then it all escalated. First my dad was the precious gift, the bicycle that was taken away from Micky. Then it was me, her son, at a safe distance in a life of his own. She put on a lot of weight and developed a kind of blank far away look on her face. Al's drinking was controllable. Micky's wasn't. He could handle it and function, one of his favorite words. She could not, not any longer. What followed were years in and out of institutional care, Betty Ford-type clinics, psychotherapy, shock treatments, and drugs to prevent drinking. After drying out and treatment, she would try. It was humiliating for her in so many ways but she knew people cared and she would try. She would be with us for awhile, able to manage a weak smile, to buy gifts for others, to make holiday celebrations, meals and plans. Underneath her dispirited, meek manner, within her wrecked small frame, I could still sense her smoldering rage.

Al always came up with the money for the treatments and the patience to stand by her. But it took its toll on him too; he drank more and he cared, except for a certain bitter sadness, less and less. He died in 1983 of complications of multiple strokes.

Eventually forced out of her job and into early retirement, my mother tried to take up new interests. But she was not a social animal, and this made the idea of Alcoholics Anonymous particularly repugnant and frightening in her mind. None of the cures, the reforms, stuck very long. She would always revert, and each time spiral a little lower. And the physical cost mounted. She knew that she was dying long before any of us understood or accepted it.

There had been many good things to remember, but mostly in her final years, there were scenes and episodes I did not want to recall. I prefer to go back to the earlier times. I was just past twelve and going out on my own to a roller-skating party at night "with real girls." I was a nervous wreck. And I told my mom and my stepdad. What would I say? How should I act? What if …? They laughed at me a little but going out the door she took my hands and, with the warmest smile, said "Just be yourself, you'll be fine." And I was. It was a great night and I could love her forever just for that. Looking back now, I can see that as much as my mother wanted to hang on to me, the best part of her always understood that she had to let me go and that it would be right.

She hadn't spoken for days when I last visited her at St. Vincent's Hospital. Not a word. I stood by her window in the hospital room looking out on the west side of Manhattan where we had once tried to begin a new life together. The nurses were changing her linen. As I turned back to her, a nurse tucked her in and fixed her pillow. Pointing to me, the nurse said with just enough condescension to have made my mother's blood boil on other days, "Now, do you know who this is? Do you recognize him?"

My mother angled her head slightly to better see me and then, with a look of contempt that would have turned the Medusa to stone, she clearly said, "Don't be ridiculous. That's my boy, Bill." Her lips quivered as the words came out. Then we all laughed. Even she laughed. It was the last sentence she ever spoke.

Despite my early failures to secure my father's service record, I continued to make sporadic and amateurish attempts to get the information. I read novels and memoirs about the air war and corresponded with the authors. Len Deighton wrote me a good letter from County Louth, Ireland. He told me that I needed my father's group and squadron number and then I might be able to contact their alumni association, if one existed. In 1982, I tried the Air Force once again, on the recommendation of a friend at work through a senior public information officer. I received a one paragraph reply with father's service serial number, bomb group, and squadron.

I stared at the paper and congratulated myself with a "Great, now what do I do with this." The years turned into a decade. I kept chipping away, messages in bottles, but nothing ever came of it except a growing sense of urgency. It wasn't even a proper avocation; it was rather something I would suddenly turn to on an impulse. The demands of family life and making a living didn't seem to be very forgiving of my secret compulsion. But it was there and the need was growing.

It was the '90s; I shared Hollywood's *Memphis Belle* with my wife and kids and the bomber episode of Steven Spielberg's *Amazing Stories.* It seemed to me that everyone under thirty-five was running around in a brown leather bomber jacket just to provoke me. All of a sudden I was fifty. The kids were almost all grown up. My oldest son, Bill, had served in the Gulf War and come home again. And still the same puzzle about my father closed in on me. I remember watching the PBS series on the Civil War and being so moved by the touching human details, the pain, the bravery, the tragedy, and the loss. So long ago had seemed so close.

Then the something I had been reaching for happened. It was October 1993 and as I read my copy of *The New York Times* I happened to come upon the obituary of a remarkable two-war American flier named Joseph Moller, who had passed away at the age of ninety-two. In WWII, Moller had headed up the 390th Bomb Group of the Eighth Air Force, and the article said that there was a memorial organization museum and library that honored his name in Tucson, Arizona. I figured, wrongly as it turned out, that the 390th must have been close to my father's group, the 392nd.

So I wrote to a director of the museum, and he, John Warner, wrote back just before Thanksgiving with a list of very specific sources to tap into and steps to take to develop information on what had happened to my father.

These included the National Archives, the Bureau of Mortuary Affairs, and the Air Force Historical Research Center, Maxwell Air Base. I was told that as next of kin and due to the Freedom of Information Act I should be able to access whatever was on file. One of the contacts John Warner listed was a Cliff Peterson in Florida. Warner said he was a kind of information coordinator for the 392nd.

On December 2, I received a voice mail message from a Jim Marsteller in Pennsylvania. He said that Peterson had faxed him a copy of my letter and then phoned Marsteller about me the same night. Marsteller later explained in a phone conversation that he had been doing extensive research on the 392nd's raid of March 18, 1944, when my father was killed, and that he had immediate information about my dad that he could share. He added that he knew all the ropes and might be able to help shave considerable time off my inquiries through official channels.

This all hit me with a gathering force of mixed emotions the strongest of which were joy, relief, and active anticipation for all that was to come. I had the immediate sense that I was starting something, and I abandoned all concern for where it might take me.

Jim Marsteller began rattling off facts, interrupted only by my eager follow-up questions. He knew, as I already did, that my dad was buried at Lorraine Cemetery, St. Avold, France and that he had received the Air Medal with oak leaf cluster and the Purple Heart. He told me dad had been stationed at Wendling, near Norwich, England. He confirmed that the group was a B24 unit of Liberators, unlike the B17s the 390th flew.

He gave me the name of dad's pilot and the name, rank, and crew assignments of the other eight airmen on his ship, which he said was J42100117, on its sixteenth mission. That mission was Friedrichshafen, Germany, on Lake Constance and the Swiss border. And he told me the nickname of the ship was "Delayed Action."

The irony of the name did not escape the listener but Marsteller kept going. He said that he had a copy of the original Missing Air Crew Report (MACR), a key document, and photocopies of the navigators roll or signed release form for their March 18, 1944 flight instructions that morning.

I recognized instantly that this was the last time my father had signed his name. My eyes blurred over as I made Jim promise to fax me that sheet. I would tell others later that at that same instant, the hairs on the back of my neck felt like they were standing on end. Time had seemed to quickly slip away, to melt. But I lied about the feeling because I worried that the truth would strain credibility, would cause people to wonder about me. For I realized that what I had felt for a few seconds was an open hand pressed against the back of my neck. It had been deliberate, insistent. Firm and cool, but in no way threatening, and then just as suddenly it was gone.

I told Jim Marsteller that I couldn't continue, and we agreed to speak later that same evening. All of a sudden I had a lot to think about, answers to questions that I had wondered about for years. Marsteller sent me the sheet with my father's scrawled signature along with those of the twenty-seven other navigators who went up that morning. There were copies too of a recent 392nd newsletter account of the Friedrichshafen raid and another about Marsteller's own fascinating story.

Marsteller and a cousin named Jim Morris both took their first names to honor their late uncle, Everett "Jim" Morris, staff sergeant and gunner on another B24 Liberator of the 392nd shot down on the Friedrichshafen raid. Morris was killed with eight more of his crew. There was one survivor.

The two Jims, Marsteller and Morris, always knew about their uncle, but some years before they had inherited a footlocker of wartime artifacts when their grandmother died. Suddenly their interest became a driving force as they set about finding out everything they could. Marsteller was particularly methodical and relentless.

In 1992, Jim Marsteller secured the complete mission file for the 392nd's sortie against Friedrichshafen. It was hundreds of pages, much of it previously classified and unseen by many veterans of the 392nd. The information allowed the 392nd newsletter to publish an account of what the group record said happened to most of the downed planes and crews on March 18, 1944.

About the time of the forty-ninth anniversary of the raid, Marsteller went to Wendling and the little German village of Hardt, near Schramberg, which was where he had determined his uncle's plane came down. Jim received a citation from the mayor and was introduced to a farmer who had been an eyewitness to the crash. The German farmer had been a young soldier home on leave then. He'd been playing with his brother in the snow on that Saturday afternoon. The B24 broke in two before hitting the ground. The youngsters ran to the site. One red headed-freckled airman was still alive. But he could only move his eyes and then he closed them forever. He was the radio operator on this ship, "Old Glory," Sgt. George Slack.

The farmer then took Marsteller to his barn and pulled out a piece of aluminum plate with faded insignia. Against orders of the military, the soldier had secreted away pieces of the wreck and Jim came back from Germany with a tangible connection to the men of the 392nd's "Old Glory." Marsteller also recruited a German graduate student while there to help him with translation and research, even after his return to the States.

Jim Marsteller had learned how his uncle died and where he had been buried afterward. I knew I could use his help to determine the same information on my father.

Marsteller also tracked down the one survivor of that crash, who spent the duration of the war as a POW. It took him almost three years to find and speak with C.C. Strickler, waist gunner. I also had reason to believe my father's plane had survivors. I hoped that eventually I could locate one who might still be alive and willing to talk.

Jim introduced me to Delmar Johnson, navigator on a third B24 lost on this fateful mission. I phoned him in California but he did not remember my father. Del was one of only two survivors from #465, piloted by Rex Johnson, no relation. He spoke of running late to the target and losing two ships in a collision just after the Channel crossing. Then they encountered remarkably accurate flak over target and without their missing fighter escort, they were hit by wave after wave of German fighter planes, ME 109s and FW 190s. He said that they had lost twelve more Liberators in about twenty minutes of virtually continuous fighter attack.

Various people over time would tell me that the 392nd's losses at Friedrichshafen were the worst suffered by a single Eighth Bomb Group on any mission in the war. I would later learn that this was not quite accurate. The Bloody 100th BG lost fifteen over Berlin on the first full scale raid on the German capital, March 6, 1944. The Eighth lost a total of sixty-nine bombers that day. The 491st would also lose fifteen B24s over Misburg/Hanover on November 26. (Some sources say sixteen.) But the worst by far was the 445th BG, which lost twenty-five attacking Kassel and Gottingen on September 27, 1944. Five more of its Liberators crash landed in allied territory.

I got in touch with Cliff Peterson to thank him for alerting Marsteller to my request. It turned out Cliff was a past national president of the 8th Air Force Historical Society and had been the pilot of a fourth Liberator shot down on the same raid. Five of his crew did not survive. The rest were interned until their liberation at the end of April 1945.

The MACR files Jim shared with me shed little detail on the fate of "Sinister Minister," #117, the Sharpe plane. The navigator on another 579th squadron plane forward of Sharpe's position, on his right wing, reported at his debriefing at Wendling that "some chutes were seen but not counted." Second Lieutenant Tausley had no more to say on the subject in the record. The 392nd newsletter summary of 1992 uses the same language and adds a footnote, that Dutch sources reported there may have been three survivors who safely parachuted and became German captives.

So, although I knew a lot more about the circumstances, I still had no grasp of what had happened to the men of #117 and where it happened.

Cliff had some untranslated captured German documents that he had obtained from the National Archives and Jim Marsteller asked his graduate student friend, Carsten Kohlmann, to do a translation. About this same time, we got to see Cliff for the first time. My oldest son, Bill Jr., was home recuperating from a bout of pneumonia and called me up to the TV room after dinner to watch a cable special on the Eighth Air Force. Midway in the program, there was Cliff Peterson speaking for the 392nd and sharing his wartime recollections. We both got a big kick out of this surprise.

My wife tracked down the thick one-volume history of the 392nd for me, *The Liberators of Wendling*, by Bob Vickers. Again, I found a lot of useful information and photos but nothing with any bearing on my father.

In mid-December 1993, Jim sent me a set of the German documents translated by Carsten. On one side of a sheet were photocopies of the original teletypes and military memos; on the back side, Carsten placed the English translation on almost a line by line equivalent.

Most of the material dealt with survivors and dead from Cliff's plane, but there was a confusing overlap that tended to mix crews from various ships together. And there seemed to be reference to two additional nearby crashes. In addition to the twelve Liberators of the 392nd that had gone down within miles of each other, other American heavy bombers had been lost in the vicinity and survivors came down wherever their chutes and the wind took them.

It was evident that Cliff's plane had crashed near the French and Swiss borders on the edge of the Black Forest, a favorite demarcation line for the Eighth pilots and navigators. The village was called Ettenheimmunster, near Freiburg and Lahr. Cliff hadn't known the exact town but one or more of his crew had pinpointed the spot independently.

Jim had alerted me to the fact that a couple of names from my dad's crew had popped up among the lists of captured and dead at this site, according to the documents. I saw the names and knew that I was close. Two of the Luftwaffe communiques reporting on crash sites back to headquarters referred to a second "machine." On the back side, in the original German version but untranslated, I spotted the clear numerals 100117. My father's plane had crashed at the same site in Ettenheimmunster.

Documents about the captured Americans requiring hospitalization for injuries, such as Cliff's copilot, also suggested that there may have been a fourth survivor from #117, but this element became something of a protracted mystery for me, one that would nag at me for many months and across thousands of miles.

It was Christmas 1993 and among the gifts under the tree from my wife, Bernadette, was a terrific book about the air war called *Round the Clock*. My oldest son also put together a scale model Liberator and presented it to me. Just after the holiday, I received a greeting card from Cliff. Tucked in the envelope was another from author-historian and 392nd vet Bob Vickers.

It simply noted that #117 had come down in the town of Ettenheimmunster, Germany. No sources, no explanation, no further detail.

It had been a bitter December, starting with howling northeasters at the beginning of the month that blossomed into a series of biting snowstorms. And the snow, unusual for the metropolitan New York area, didn't go away. It sat there and grew, all the way to March. Two days before New Year's my feet went out from under me and I shot in the air like a fouled place kicker, loudly cracking the back of my head on the snowy pavement. I opened my eyes to see a white-haired old man staring down at me with an amused expression. "I really heard that," he said into my face. I answered up to him, "So did I."

I waited for responses to my official government inquiries. What I had learned so far was gratifying, but also tantalizing. I was eager, almost feverish to learn more. But I was also receiving a general education about what it had been like back then and was being exposed to men who had fought the war alongside my father, men who breathed life into the history. I had been self-conscious at first at making inquiries. But at every turn, the men of The Mighty Eighth treated me like one of their own and talked to me naturally, without the slightest concern that my curiosity was strange or morbid in any way. I would have to learn to be patient and to take heart. I would play out the string until it led me where I had to go.

Maybe I had needed a crack on the head to bring me back down to earth and to prepare for the rapidly approaching fiftieth anniversary of the mission.

Book II
Winds of March

Aboard the "Sinister Minister," Lieutenant McGuire tried to keep his mind on his work, but he kept drifting back to the collision. John Feran was his friend and now, unless there had been a miracle, he was scattered with his fellow airmen like so much dead meat all over the French countryside. Dust to dust, ashes to ashes, he thought.

His mind wandered back to that day John had talked him into accompanying him and John's bombardier, Howard Bjork, to Kings Lynn on a shopping mission. That was before the flak took part of Howard's jaw away. John had been enamored of this girl in Topeka just before they went east. She was a pretty young woman. Marion, that was her name. As the combat days wore on, this brief romance kept taking on bigger and bigger significance for Lt. Feran. Bill wasn't sure if it was the passion of their continuing correspondence or some sudden fear on John's part that someone back home might steal Marion away. In any case, John suddenly determined he had to get the lady a set of rings and, when McGuire and Bjork failed to convince him that he may be acting a tad impetuously, they agreed to tag along.

The three of them stared down at the counter at three sets of rings, two gold and one platinum. The eager jewel merchant sought to hurry things along by periodically clearing his throat. John looked like he would stand there all day, so Bill said: "The ladies find platinum quite fashionable these days." That did it!

Within a couple of weeks from the day of the purchase, Marion sent Lt. Feran a "Dear John" letter. Bill wondered where the rings were and what would happen to them now. It had all been so important that day, a matter of life and death. Then he pushed it all away.

Unplugging his oxygen line and grabbing a walk-around oxygen bottle, the Navigator got up from his table and moved forward into the nose. He crouched under Richardson in the turret and stretched out prone on his belly. Looking out and to his right through the plexiglass nose he saw the rest of the first group of the 392nd, their contrails streaking white on the bright blue sky. Below, he spotted the ribbon of the Rhine and its broad flat plain. Further right, and south, he could plainly see a section of the Alps. Despite all the circumstances of war, the sheer fascination of flying still held him in its mysterious grip. As he made his way back to his station, he said one word aloud, "Awesome."

On the opposite end of the formation, waist gunner Bode on "The Doodle Bug" was separating packets of thin foil strip chaff and tossing them out the window. "Not going to fool anyone," he told himself, as he did it. "They don't need any radar to see us coming today." But Bode also knew that the chaff might just be enough to keep the Germans from getting an accurate altitude fix, and that could make all the difference in the world once the ack-ack fire found them.

In the copilot's seat on "El Lobo," Major Keilman, the mission leader, had much the same idea about their visibility, as he fretted over fighter coverage and the delay to the IP or initial point. He felt that the formation was a little ragged but OK, given the circumstances of the earlier collision. Lieutenant Kale in "Li'l Gypsy," #127, in the high squadron slot, seemed to be experiencing some mechanical difficulties and was straggling some on the right. The planned bomb run called for them to fly east past the primary target and then come around back from the east end of Lake Constance, the Bodensee, the IP, for the final twenty miles to bombs away. Absent fighter support, Keilman believed that they were as ready as they were going to be.

Behind and above "El Lobo," in #981, "Big Time Operator," leading the high squadron, engineer Hinshaw listened to the familiar voice of their radio operator, Gene Rosko. Rosko was in regular contact with Lieutenant Peterson. The engineer and the radio man were alike, Hinshaw reasoned, in that they both had a great interest in how things worked. As a result of this leaning and his aptitude, Hinshaw had taught him a lot about his own job, and Rosko functioned as a kind of unofficial assistant. He was not only better at it, thought Hinshaw, but he was also closer at hand than the rest of the crew. The two even spent their free time together tinkering with metal scraps in the base machine shop. They fashioned all kinds of gadgets, making rough Bowie knives and salt and pepper shakers from shell casings. To Hinshaw, Rosko was solid stuff.

Looking down over Lake Constance, Hinshaw now noticed some thin clouds and patches of dirtier smoke over the water. He knew this was from the smudge pots on barges that the Germans set out to try to obscure the city. The blue of the water struck him as deep, calm, ancient, and unreal. He almost wanted to be angry at it but he knew that would be foolish.

In the lead of the second group, pilot Don Clover, and copilot "Bob" Berger, were at the controls of "The Jungle Princess," #411, for the twenty-second time, though not exactly. They had lost the real "Princess" some time before but for this crew, whatever they flew was "The Jungle Princess." Farther back on the ship, waist gunner James Ross looked out on Switzerland and dreamed of his native Scotland. Less than twenty-four hours earlier he had kissed his mother goodbye there, after a short leave at home. He'd signed up with the Yanks to bring the war to the enemy and now he found himself through the wonders of modern transportation doing exactly that. From his doorstep to theirs in one day.

"The Princess" carried an extra navigator, on his first mission for orientation purposes. "El Lobo," leading the 392nd, also carried a pilotage navigator/nose gunner, who was trained to spot landmarks as a navigational aide. Sitting in the "Lobo" nose turret, Lieutenant Stupski heard Major Keilman give a verbal command for the ninety degree turn and then they banked to the right. Soon another, and they were at the I P and beginning the bomb run. Stupski was the first to see the flak up ahead.

On "The Princess," copilot Bob Berger repeated pilot Don Clover's order as it was executed. "Bomb bay doors coming open," and the pilot told bombardier Paul McDonald that his instruments were now in control of the ship. This action was repeated at more or less the same instant throughout the formation.

Major Keilman didn't think the anti-aircraft barrage from the Germans' magnificent 88's was all that bad. They'd certainly flown through worse before. He had hardly completed the thought when the barrage seemed to engulf them and "El Lobo" began to buck and rattle from the impact of the exploding charges. To add to the confusion, the 44th Bomb Group pulled out of the formation, forced to make a slow turn by the encroachment of still another bomber unit on their own bomb run. The 44th would circle and try again, but the 392nd plowed on through the clouds of deadly flak. Keilman knew his group was next to last in the formation and the delays, and now the absence of the 44th in the lead, meant that the 392nd was virtually alone over Germany. Suddenly a loud hit brought immediate loss of altitude and speed. Baumgart told him they must have lost their number four engine to the flak and feathered it, turning the propeller blades edgewise into the slip stream. The pilot applied full throttle to the remaining engines but they rapidly lost more speed and position, with the rest of the formation running past them. Bombardier White tried to adjust but it was too late. "El Lobo" would miss the drop.

As #465 in the low squadron lead started the run, navigator Del Johnson heard someone on the interphone cry out to pilot Rex

Johnson and suddenly, the ship pulled violently to the left. Looking over his shoulder, Del saw the whole formation veering left.

"The Jungle Princess" engineer was shouting from the top turret, "Collision course. One o'clock," and pilot Don Clover, declutching the AFCE automatic flight control system and taking control back from the bombardier, banked sharply left. The 392nd was under another formation with bomb bay doors open and bombs about to be released. The other group of American bombers had come in from above, on the right. The Wendling group's second contingent, though in imminent jeopardy, managed to get far enough over so that only a couple of planes were exposed, and the bombs passed through without damage, even as the flak barrage continued all around them. "The Jungle Princess" was forced to seek a new target of opportunity. Since it was too late for their primary target, they would have to zero in on another suitable objective.

Anti-aircraft shells, those deadly puffs of dirty cotton that completely surrounded them, were badly damaging the 392nd. "Li'l Gypsy," #127, made the drop but took several hits and lost their number one engine. Lt. Kale took her down under the formation and told his crew they could do no better than Switzerland. "Gypsy" cut across the line of Liberators, heading directly south.

In the top turret of "Big Time Operator," #981, engineer Hinshaw couldn't help remembering the effect of flak damage on the ground crews back at Wendling. How they would bitch and moan about what a miserable life they had on the line working all night in all kinds of weather to prepare the B24s, while the fliers, they said, slept in their warm bunks and ate special food. Hah! Until the planes came back and they looked under the fuselages and saw the flak holes. That always shut them up.

Suddenly, another concussion and jolt. The ship had taken several hits and now pilot Peterson lost an engine. Their bombs had hit the target but #981 was paying a price. Again, a crunching buffet as "Big Time Operator" took one on the nose. Hinshaw's full attention went to his gauges to check for any indications of fuel leakage.

Shards of red-hot metal banged into and sliced open the Libs as they released their bombs and pushed on west. On #117, Lieutenant Sharpe felt a sharp pain and reached with a jerk for his right arm. The blood on his hand seemed oddly distant but the numbing pain made him gasp. Copilot Bandura tried to help him, as they asked for damage reports from the rest of the "Sinister Minister" crew.

An 88 millimeter shell blew through the nose behind the navigator on "El Lobo," but it did not explode. It left two dinner plate size holes in the nose and floor of the mission leader. In the rear contingent, #692 on Clover's right wing lost number three engine and suffered heavy flak damage. Pilot Walter Hebron asked navigator Leo McDonald for a heading for Switzerland and peeled off the formation.

On #371, "The Doodle Bug," tail end Charlie for the 392nd, waist gunner John Bode whistled to himself as they ricocheted their way through the worst flak concentration they had ever seen. None of the bursts were off the formation. The Germans were zeroed in.

Just then, another explosion rocked the ship, with fragments hitting their bombardier in the face. Bode heard him screaming incoherently over the interphone.

In the lead slot, Lt. George Spartage in #990 saw the command ship "El Lobo" trailing smoke and then he saw the fighters. Aboard "El Lobo," both Baumgart's waist gunners called out to him simultaneously, "Fighters at three o'clock." Over thirty Messerschmitt 109s, in close formation, paralleled the Libs course on the right, but were climbing rapidly. Major Keilman used the command radio to call for their own fighters.

The Messerschmitts closed in, turned and dove in successive lines of five or six abreast, wings almost touching, at speeds approaching 500 miles an hour. Firing. Then they would break away or cut right through to form up for another pass.

Waist gunner Chester Strickler on Lt. Dallas Books' "Old Glory," in the deputy lead position, struggled to keep himself under control, concentrating on the enemy's lightning quick passes. He led the target with his fire, squeezing off short bursts, just as he had been trained but he felt like he was standing on the edge of hell. The other waist gunner was dead at his feet, and the ball turret gunner had been killed as well.

By the time they'd dropped their bombs, "Old Glory" had already been badly damaged and then the fighters started. Tail gunner Sgt. Daniel Jones was now trapped in the turret which had been set aflame by enemy fire. The fire had spread rapidly. Strickler could not get him free or stop the fire. Jones kept calling out to him, calling his nickname. "Pappy," he called, "help me." But there was nothing Strickler could do.

The fighters had set their number four afire as "Old Glory" tried an evasive left-hand turn out over Lake Constance. Strickler saw parts of the plane tearing off and flying past the waist window. The gunner called pilot Books and argued for Switzerland. Books kept struggling, trying to get the plane under control. He said, "Hold it a minute…we'll be all right."

Rex Johnson could not slow #465 down enough to stay with the formation without stalling, after they had veered left to avoid colliding with another group of heavy bombers. So they shot ahead and bombed the target alone. They circled until the low block caught up, and then fell into the back of the group.

Through the astrodome, the navigator's celestial observation window, Del Johnson saw a formation of Focke Wulf 190s swing in just ahead. He called them off on the interphone to help his gunners as the Germans rose up and dove into their attack. Del saw one fighter whiz past as he crouched behind the armor of the nose turret. For an instant, he thought it had completely missed them. But then a missile, trailing sparks and fire, roared through the nose turret and exploded in the pilot's compartment behind. #465 immediately began to spiral down sharply.

Lt. Peterson on "Big Time Operator" ordered engineer Hinshaw to go forward and check out the nose. "It's too damn cold in here," Peterson said. "Something's wrong." Rosko took Hinshaw's place in the turret.

Hinshaw crawled down into the nose with a bail out bottle tube stuck in his mask. The nose was a mess. The nose wheel door was open and frigid air blew into the cabin with gale force. Their recently acquired navigator had evidently taken it upon himself to bail out through the nose wheel hatch. Hinshaw made his way toward the sealed nose turret. He opened the heavy turret door and saw their bombardier's back slumped over the guns. Ed Brown's dead body fell into his arms. He had a deep head wound.

As another wave of fighters pulled away from the second group of the 392nd, Lieutenant Elsworth Anderson's #824, in the lead slot position, exploded in flames. Three chutes descended with the wreckage.

"The Doodle Bug's" Bode knew a fighter was on her tail but he couldn't do anything about it. The tail gunner was returning fire but his guns kept jamming sporadically.

"Hard to Get," #518, on Cliff Peterson's right wing, peeled off from the formation while under furious fighter attack. As the fighters continued their onslaught, "Hard to Get," perhaps in desperation, began a nearly impossible outside loop, or roll maneuver.

Bode looked out "The Doodle Bug's" waist door to see a B24 flying upside down. Then he spotted an ME109 about 300 feet below in pursuit. It seemed to assume that the "Bug" was dead or abandoned. Bode opened up his guns, point blank. The engine sprayed glycol and the fighter spun away, smoking. Out of control, it continued rapidly descending toward the ground. Bode knew he had killed the pilot.

"Hard to Get" exploded after completing its fantastic loop. One chute fell away safely. John Bode saw the remains of five Liberators, trailing smoke as they fell to earth like the long gnarled fingers of a ghostly hand. As they helped remove their blinded bombardier from the nose turret, the crew of "The Doodle Bug" saw another forty fighters approaching, ME109s and FW190s, at three o'clock. They stood off and fired. White puffs of smoke appeared around the ship. They were time-release charges, but none seemed to hit. The fighters then pulled out ahead and dove into a frontal attack, cutting through the remains of the formation.

A 20mm cannon shell exploded in the navigator's instrument panel on the mission leader, "El Lobo." Metal fragments caught the navigator's face and left eye. The waist gunners reported three Liberators going down and Major Keilman again radioed repeatedly for fighter cover.

Flying just ahead of "Doodle Bug," on the right, was Lt. George Haffermehl's "The Arsenal," #826. Damaged, and under continuing attack, he fell away from the formation near the Swiss-German border.

Haffermehl gave the order to bail out and left the plane. Waist gunner F. J. Wagner didn't get out until they were about 500 feet over the ground. He was killed in the bail out attempt.

"The Arsenal" copilot, Don McMullen, decided to stay with the plane and regained enough control for a crash landing. Their badly wounded bombardier, the navigator, and the ball turret gunner had also remained aboard. McMullen put the plane safely down just south of the Rhine in Switzerland.

As he passed #100, "Double Trouble," Captain Baumgart on "El Lobo" looked out and saw a big hole in the cockpit window where the copilot's head should have been. "Double Trouble" was heavily damaged, a flying wreck. The bomb bay doors were open and hooked onto them, a white chute flapped forlornly. There were no signs of life.

But aboard Lieutenant J. E. Muldoon's "Double Trouble," there was quite a lot going on. A 20mm shell had come through the window just behind the copilot's head and exploded in the radio compartment. It set the radio operator's parachute on fire and the crew couldn't put the fire out. They flung the chute out the bomb bay, but it snagged and continued to burn. The fire then shorted out the bail out bell, causing it to ring. The bombardier and navigator, hearing the alarm in the nose, both bailed out and were killed.

The rest of the crew realized the ship was intact, with all four engines running, and stayed aboard. Finally, they managed to put out the fire, and stumbled back toward the Channel.

On #465, navigator Del Johnson pulled the emergency handles to open the nose wheel doors. He quickly stripped off his flak armor and checked the seat chute pack he always chose to wear. He disconnected the earphones and throat microphone, unplugged the flying suit heating cord and the oxygen mask hose, and tossed away his steel battle helmet. As he crouched down to exit, all four engines seemed to come to life again. Pausing, he waited to see if the plane would right itself, from the slow spiral it was falling in, and level off. But the engines slowed again and the spiral continued. Johnson, aided by the centrifugal force that at first resisted his effort to escape, shot out of the Liberator like a champagne cork.

But the spiraling B24, moving at about 190 miles per hour, was coming around after him. He jerked the ripcord and was pulled back up as the edge of the right wing, outboard of the props, struck his left ankle.

He floated then, in near perfect silence. He watched the 392nd's ragged formation going off in the distance. He barely heard the murmur of machine gun fire, fleeting and muted, like the rapidly dissipating memory of a bad dream. And there was the world coming up to meet him, faster and faster.

On "Old Glory," Chester Strickler was still at his post, fighting off fighters, but he was the only one left alive in the rear of the plane. The fire and smoke were growing impossible and he knew Lt. Books didn't have a clear picture of the extent of their problem. Books still struggled with the controls. Strickler heard their navigator, Captain John Slowik, on the interphone cursing the Germans and repeating that he didn't want to go down. The gunner saw the second fire on the right wing creeping into the roots of the fuselage.

He started to call Books once more when the fighters swung into them again. His oxygen mask was shot away. Cannon shells exploded everywhere, but he continued to fire his guns. There was a sudden explosion as a shell hit a tank of pressurized oxygen. The force of the blast hurled him like a rag doll through the waist door and out into open space.

Chester Strickler was free falling at 18,000 feet, blissfully unconscious. When he awoke, he struggled to close the second clip of his parachute pack onto the chute harness. Then he reached for the ripcord D ring. Where was the D ring? He grabbed for it frantically. Weakened by his ordeal and the lack of oxygen, Strickler fell almost three miles before his chute safely opened and landed him in Germany. From his airborne perch, he saw "Old Glory" explode and come down in two great pieces. There were no chutes. He was the sole survivor.

"El Lobo" was not in good shape. Captain Baumgart stared through the cockpit window at the blood covered face of his navigator. From the plexiglass bubble of the astrodome, Lt. Connelly stared back at him with a dazed expression and kept trying to wipe the blood from his face with his hands.

Then the pilotage navigator, Lt. Stupski, began screaming over the interphone that the entire nose floor was covered in blood. "… And Lieutenant White (the bombardier) is trying to throw Connelly out of the plane."

With a little help from the engineer, some sanity was soon restored. It was quickly determined that one of the hydraulic lines had been severed by a shell, leaking red hydraulic fluid all over the deck. Shocked and nearly blinded, the wounded navigator had started to bail out. Lt. White was forcibly trying to restrain him and Stupski misinterpreted this struggle. A shot of morphine helped to calm Lt. Connelly down and ease his pain.

Lieutenant Peterson had successfully avoided two heavy fighter attacks. The third, however, would prove to be "Big Time Operator's" final engagement. Peterson, and one B24 on his left wing, were now all that was left of the high squadron. A heavy bomber relied on in-flight adjustment of ailerons, elevators, and rudder to help trim, or balance, and steer the ship. When these tabs, or controls failed, the pilot was forced to compensate for the added strain on the stick with his own muscle as best he could.

Engineer Hinshaw knew now that the trim tabs would no longer trim #981 and that their pilot, a big man, held the controls through sheer brute strength. In dread, the Peterson crew watched the forty German fighters circle again and form up ahead. Then they soared down on the Liberator in still another frontal attack. Hinshaw shot big chunks off of one of them. The German fighter skimmed over his top turret and crashed into #981's vertical stabilizers, shearing off large sections of metal. The Lib immediately shot into a near vertical spiral dive. It was time to bail out.

As Cliff Peterson and copilot Russ Vreiling started to leave their seats, they could look to the right and clearly see number three engine turning. The entire right side of the cockpit had been blown out. When it went, Lt. Peterson looked up for a split second to see a German fighter pilot's face as he sped by. Peterson didn't know if he was alive or dead, or why he had passed so dangerously close to the damaged Lib.

They hit the alarm bell and Vreiling yelled, "Let's get the hell out of here." Both of them were bleeding from shrapnel and glass. They all had backpack chutes on already. They stopped at the top turret. Hinshaw's legs and feet dangled limply from above. Both bloody faces stared at each other, unbelieving. They vigorously began to shake the engineer's legs and to pull him down from his seat, when miraculously, he came back to life. "Something must have hit me," he said. They realized he was in better shape than they were. "Not a scratch," said Peterson.

The three of them quickly headed for the bomb bay. They couldn't get the big doors open, due in part to the angle and force of their descent. Jumping, kicking, and stomping together, they eventually did force them open and, joined by radio operator Rosko, safely chuted from the doomed #981.

At about 1520 hours, Lt. Walter Hebron dumped his bombsight into the Bodensee and #692 descended toward Swiss air space. He lowered his landing gear as a Swiss ME 109 joined them for escort into Dubendorf Airfield. After a successful emergency landing, all eleven occupants were interned by the Swiss Army.

In the fighter attacks, the pilot, copilot, and navigator of the "Sinister Minister," #117, were wounded. The ship was afire and began to go down as the formation approached the edge of the Black Forest and the Rhine. She exploded on impact.

Aboard Spartage's #990, navigator Tausley recorded the approximate time and coordinates for #117. He noted in the log: "Some chutes seen but not counted."

Lieutenant Bruce Sooy's "Pink Lady," #945, which flew the low slot position behind Rex Johnson, also saw one fighter attack too many. He successfully crash landed a little northeast of #117. His ten-man crew was captured and held by the Germans for the duration of the war.

Lieutenant Lynn Peterson's "Old Daddy" was last seen under heavy fighter attack at approximately 1530 hours over the Colmar-Vosges region of France. This Liberator, #497, had led the second unit low squadron. Now it circled away from the formation and spun down to a crash. First, four chutes were seen. Then, three more. Three never made it.

Eventually the fighter support, or Little Friends, that Major Keilman had kept calling for showed up. The Big Friends, the heavy bombers that remained, were glad to see the P47s, P38s and P51s join in for the rest of the trip. But like jackals, the enemy fighters continued to harass the wounded 392nd at every opportunity.

Twin-engined JU 88s tailed "El Lobo" just out of range of the formation's guns. The damaged Lib trailed the group now in the tail end Charlie position. The German fighter-bombers commenced firing and Captain Baumgart veered first one way, then another. With each turn, white puffs appeared next to the B24. More exploding 30mm. time- fused shells. Then, apparently out of ammunition, the Germans broke off the attack.

After hitting what they thought was a marshaling yard, "The Jungle Princess" rejoined the formation and battled through two fighter attacks, but succumbed to a third. There were too many solid hits, and fires quickly engulfed the Lib. They knew the drill and all eleven bailed out successfully. As Don Clover hit the silk, this latest "Princess" blew sky high. The men were widely scattered in the snow between Colmar and Strasbourg and eventually all were captured by the German occupation force.

Tiefendal, #989, "Son of Satan," made it only as far as Gravesend, Kent. Two of his crew were dead. On only two engines, Lieutenant William E. Meighan brought "The Doodle Bug" into Biggin Hill, another RAF base in Kent, after dumping everything they could into the Channel to maintain altitude. The rest of the battle-scarred 392nd, the sad remnants of a once proud force, set down at Wendling more than nine hours after takeoff. The mood on the base was somber, a kind of shock that hung over them all for days. While working on "El Lobo" late that first night back, the ground crew counted one- hundred-and-forty-seven holes in the Liberator's metal frame.

In December 1993, I had written my father's three sisters and surviving two brothers to tell them about my research efforts and what I had learned so far.

Some weeks later I spoke with the older brother, Uncle Jim, and then I received a nice letter from Virginia from Uncle Gerry. Gerry was a young teenager when my father was killed in 1944. Included, he explained, were copies of a "V Mail" letter that Bill had sent his little brother in January 1944.

"V Mail" was a system that microfiched G.I. correspondence onto a huge reel which was then economically shipped to the States. It involved a standardized short form for writing space. On the other side of the Atlantic, the microfiche film was processed to produce a hard copy for local delivery.

This was the first time that I had ever seen or read any words of my father's. In the letter, he closes with a paragraph that attempts to explain the war in simple terms to his kid brother at home. In so doing, in my eyes, he spoke to the very reasons he believed he was there. To me now, there was no doubt that my father knew exactly what he was fighting for and what was at risk. The letter became an instant prize possession and I was grateful to my uncle for giving it to me after holding it for so long.

I was very proud of it, saying to my wife: "You know, I'd rather have this piece of old paper than a box full of medals they might have given him."

About that time, I also received some forms to fill out from the National Archives in response to my earlier request for information. Credit cards were accepted to cover shipping and fees, etc. They explained that the proper file had been identified and that documents would be copied and shipped once the forms were sent in … "in two or three months." I had an image of that scene at the end of the film, *Raiders of the Lost Ark,* where the camera kept pulling back and back to reveal more and more rows of dusty archives in a warehouse of Pentagonian proportions. I filled out the forms and sent them off, still hoping against hope that I would have all the information before the anniversary of the raid.

What I really wanted, needed, was a live witness. I had yet to come in contact with anyone from the 392nd who had actually known or remembered my father. My hope was more ambitious, that I could find a survivor of #117 who would talk to me. In early January, I received a letter from Jim Goar in Indiana, the editor of the 392nd newsletter. The letter closed with a well intentioned and well stated sentiment:

> *If some time you are close, or even if you're not, you would probably enjoy coming to one of our reunions. You would*

*probably never meet a man who actually knew your father,
but the men you would talk to would be practical
substitutes and some could be the personification of your
father had he lived.*

I was after more than that, a lot more. I knew that I had
enough determination to track down a survivor, but I could not be
sure, in the end, if that was possible. It was the surest path, however,
to knowing what happened to #117.

I thought waist gunner Carl Anderson a likely survivor, based
on the documents I had seen so far. My uncle Hugh Breslin, a
retired Air Force major, wrote suggesting an ad in the back of
Retired Officer magazine. The whole process would take some
months but we went ahead. There was also the route Jim Marsteller
had taken to get in touch with Chester Strickler from his uncle's
plane. That involved locating the right state veterans chapter for
Anderson and then forwarding a blind letter through them, hoping
he might respond.

But out of the blue, later that January, an answer arrived in
the mail. A letter from the Air Force Historical Research Agency
at Maxwell Air Force Base in Alabama contained two enclosures
in response to my November request. One piece was an excerpt,
stamped secret/declassified, from the 392nd BG history. This turned
out to be another contemporary account of the Friedrichshafen
mission. The second document had a similarly stamped cover sheet
identifying it as part of the 579th Bomb Squadron history. The
attached page was a list of the #117 crew with their 1944 home
addresses.

I circled the names and addresses of the four airmen I thought
possible survivors. Armed with this 50-year-old lead, I began calling
the information directory service at each location. My first two
tries came up empty: no listing for that name.

The third was a Michael Cugini or Gugini - - spelled differently in various documents. The Buffalo, N.Y., operator had a listing at a different address in a suburb that sounded like Chicawanga. I tried the number. A woman answered and I launched into my rapid fire routine, trying not to think about how strange it must sound. Then there was an awkward silence. Finally, she said, "But who are you?"

In my haste, I thought that maybe I had skipped over that key element. I told her. "Sure," she replied, "I knew your father. And I knew your mom, too."

Arlene Cugini was courted by and married to Michael before he went overseas, and she went out to visit him in training in Kansas, Topeka, and Salina. There was a long impatient pause as she struggled to remember the second town's name. She explained that her husband was out at that moment. "I could tell you the story of what happened to them," she went on, "Lord knows I've heard it often enough." But she knew Michael would want to tell it all himself. I got their home address before breaking off.

A day went by without that call. The next day, I express-mailed a letter, once again explaining who I was and what I was looking for. I included copies of some documents I thought Cugini would be interested in. I closed by asking for a call or a written response.

But there was no response. On the Friday of Super Bowl weekend, more than two weeks after speaking with Arlene Cugini, I called their home once again. There was a recorded message from Michael saying he wasn't available. I dutifully left a short message of my own with my phone number.

That Thursday I had also received a big padded envelope from the National Archives. Inside was one roughly 4 by 5 inch strip of film card in its own paper sleeve. That was it. No cover letter, no instructions, no explanation. The microfiche showed some eighty-four exposures, each smaller than a thumb nail. They were impossible to decipher but each seemed to represent a one page document.

Being unfamiliar with microfiche, I gave it to my friend Tun Aung, an art director, who was going to have enlarged prints made on one big piece of photo paper.

That Saturday afternoon, while my wife was working at the library and I was doing some cooking and watching Seton Hall lose to Boston College on TV, Michael Cugini finally returned my calls.

He began with an apology, explaining that he had had a heart attack several weeks before. He had been lying low, he said, particularly given the snowy weather. He had a soft, light voice with that unmistakable close-to-Canada upstate New York twang in it. It felt easy to talk to him, but a little awkward as well.

Cugini confirmed most of the basic facts as I understood them. He said that #117 was on its return leg, just minutes after the bombing, when the fighters came, but he remembered it as one long attack. He said there was a fire under the fuselage and the front of the plane had been badly shot up. Three of them decided it was time to go. "It wasn't official or anything," he offered. The replacement ball turret Covenez went right away, Cugini a little later, and Anderson last. As far as he knew, Maylander in the tail and all the rest stayed at their stations. "There wasn't time," he said. "There just wasn't any time."

I did not want to press the older man. I just wanted to let him talk and keep him talking. I asked him if he knew where he landed. Cugini didn't have a clue. "It could have been Switzerland for all I knew," he responded. He said he did see other chutes but hardly noticed. "It all happened too quickly," he added.

In his only reference to captivity, Cugini asked me if I had been able to contact Anderson. I explained that I hadn't. Cugini said that while he was a POW, he had seen Anderson in another compound and knew that he had survived. He told me that after the war, he had tried to track him down in Iowa and heard that he had moved to Michigan. But he couldn't find him. There was a sadness in his voice.

My letter had described a photo I had of eight crew men in flying suits posed, in two rows, in front of the narrow waist of a B17. My dad was the only one I knew. Cugini explained on the phone that this was the crew of #117 during training in the southwest, maybe Tucson, in June or July 1943. A base photographer offered to shoot them. The only plane close at hand was a B17 Fortress. Two of the guys were off somewhere, but the picture was taken. He said he had a copy in his scrapbook.

My Uncle Gerry's letter to me had also mentioned that he didn't know exactly how he knew, but he distinctly remembered that the name of brother Bill's Liberator was not "Delayed Action" but "Sinister Minister." Cugini now volunteered the same information in no uncertain terms. He said he never heard the name "Delayed Action" until he read it in my letter.

Michael Cugini said that serving with the men of #117 was "the best time in my life." He said there was a real good feeling among all of them, officers and men. They did everything and went everywhere together, he said. "Your dad, he always kept us in line. He always got us home."

"I wanna tell you something," he told me. "And I'm not just saying this to boost you up or anything. Of all of them," he continued, "your dad was the one each of us liked best. I don't know what it was. Maybe because he was older. But we all looked up to him."

Cugini then said that he didn't think my father had suffered, that in the end, they had all died quickly. That was the way Mike had sealed it in his mind.

It was a pleasant but emotionally charged conversation for both of us. We agreed to talk again. I said I might want to come up to Buffalo and see him if that was all right. Without hesitation, he said they would be happy to see me.

The enlargement of the microfiche was still too small to be of any use. My wife again came to the rescue, with the simple revelation to me that there was a microfiche viewer and printer in the basement of the town library. "Eureka," was my response.

But the documents proved to be of poor quality. Most were very faint impressions. A good number were totally illegible. Photocopies were, of course, worse. Most of the papers were captured original German military records and communications, which had been translated. Of the eighty-four pages I reviewed and took notes from, I photocopied some fifty-three. The material was not exclusive to #117, but covered Bruce Sooy's plane, #945, and Cliff Peterson's #981 as well. I was already familiar with some of the Peterson material through Marsteller and Kohlmann. There was some overlap and duplication, but I also had the sense that some material might have simply been misplaced.

Among the minutia was a hospital admission report dated March 24, 1944, from St. Agnes Reserve Hospital II, Freiburg. Among the eight prisoners referenced were Sgt. Chester Strickler, being treated for "fracture of left lower leg" and 1st Lt. Delmar Johnson for "fracture of left lower leg and contusion of right knee." Both admitted March 19, 1944.

Another piece of paper referenced the name Masters. It was a report of Ettenheimmunster officials that July saying "berry pickers" in the local woods had come upon the body of an American aviator. He was buried in the local cemetery.

Concerning #117, the file said a Nalton Maylander was identified by the Germans at the crash site and declared dead. After that the information was sketchy and hard to decipher. Many planes had gone down, possibly three in this one area. It was difficult at times to see which plane was being referenced and, as they did in the case of POWs, the Germans mixed up the dead from various crews. The remains themselves could not be identified in every case. Identity tags were missing or became misplaced. Death in hospital was another possibility.

At first, there was no reference to the pilot or copilot. The two waist gunners, Cugini and Anderson, were listed among the POWs. Clarence Covenez, belly gunner, showed up as a POW at a different site, among the wounded. On the final Missing Air Crew Report (MACR) in the file, there were marginal notations next to the three above names: "EUS" on the left, and "RTD" on the right. I interpreted this to mean something about going stateside and Returned to Duty.

On the same MACR, the pilot, copilot, TT gunner Ralph Huffman and radio operator Frank Wallace carried the designation "DED" in the margin. Adding to the confusion, Maylander in the tail; Frank Richardson, bombardier; and McGuire, the navigator, all bore a "KIA" notation.

One page from Ettenheimmunster dated either March 31 or March 21, 1944 listed the status, according to the Germans, of nine of the crew of #117 - - all but Covenez, who was held elsewhere and was not yet associated with the Ettenheimmunster crashes. It listed six dead, including Sharpe, Bandura, Richardson, Maylander, Huffman, and Wallace. Not dead, according to this document, were Anderson, Cugini, and McGuire. I tried to take this in with the grain of salt it seemed to deserve. But I could not dismiss the possibility that my father had not died on #117 after all.

Finally, Wallace's name showed up on three different documents as wounded and in hospital. March 20. March 25 or 28. March 31. The last showed him transferred from Strasbourg hospital. In all three cases, the serial number listed did not correspond to his number in U.S. records. It was also inconsistent with anyone else on the crew of #117.

If Wallace was alive on March 31, how did he show up dead on the final MACR report and when did he die?

The most valuable information in the file were debriefing sheets filled out by POW Anderson after his liberation from the German prison camp in April 1945. These were fill- in-the-blanks forms. Anderson's concise history followed the outline provided to me by Mike Cugini in all major respects save one. Cugini had told me that the navigator had been wounded or shot at the same time as the pilot and copilot. The Anderson form did not contain that information. It also seemed to indicate that the remaining seven fliers on #117 were at their stations when the plane crashed.

I rapidly built up my own file of information on the strategy, tactics, and weapons of the air war. It was apparent early on that the B24 Liberator was at a distinct disadvantage to the Flying Fortress, the B17, when it came to handling the German air defenses.

First of all, B24s were more erratic to control and difficult to fly so they provided a much less stable gunnery platform to combat fighter attack. Aerodynamics also forced them to fly in slightly looser formations than the Forts. Although originally designed to fly higher than the B17, adaptations forced so much extra weight onto the Libs they soon were required to fly at a lower ceiling than the Fortresses. All this not only made them vulnerable to enemy flak, but it also gave the German fighters increased opportunity. The joke among B17 crews on combined missions was that the presence of the B24s was the best defense they had.

I learned too, that flak was a much more insidiously effective weapon than Hollywood ever portrayed it to be. The anti-aircraft explosions in the air in the grainy old war footage had always reminded me of Chinese ideograms or characters, smudged little warrior men. But these exploding shards of metal routinely maimed and killed U.S. Army Air Forces personnel, and brought down planes.

By the beginning of 1944, Hitler was convinced that the only way to stop the daylight bombing was with more and better radar-guided FLAK, from the German, fliegerabwehrkanone. An approximate force of one million people was then assigned to this German air defense system. A larger portion of the armament budget was devoted to developing and fielding more sophisticated radar tracking.

All my reading was giving me a deeper understanding of the air war in the European Theater and the pivotal role of the Eighth Air Force. In the early months, as the Bomber Command built up its force and tested its tactics against the Germans, operations had not been nearly as effective as had been expected. Losses were also frighteningly high. The British remained loudly skeptical of the very idea of daylight bombing, which had been tried and dropped by both the RAF and the Luftwaffe. The Americans, on the other hand, had evolved a commitment to this kind of warfare over a long period of time, particularly among their senior leadership.

Things came to a head in January 1943, and General Ira Eaker, the commander of the Eighth, at General Hap Arnold's instruction, was forced to present a final argument to Winston Churchill defending the daylight concept and the ultimate autonomy of the U.S. operation. He boiled it all down to a one page memo which he handed to the Prime Minister. In describing the cooperative punch of the British night raids and American daytime offensive, he used the phrase "round the clock" destruction of

Germany, and Churchill's eyes lit up. He savored those words, "round the clock." Eaker won his case. But in the beginning of 1944 Eisenhower brought in General Carl Spaatz to command all air operations and Spaatz took Eaker out of the Eighth, sending him to head up operations in Italy. He was replaced by the famed and pugnacious Jimmy Doolittle.

While the express goal of the U.S. bombing was to cripple German war industry and its supporting infrastructure, the actual focus was the total eradication of German air power to prepare for the invasion of France and ultimately of Germany itself. While Eaker's leadership stressed this objective, the stakes had been raised at the start of 1944. U.S. claims of downed enemy fighters were proven to be wildly exaggerated, and the Germans had refined their attack tactics and beefed up their fighter force. The invasion was coming. There wasn't a lot of time left. General Doolittle was blunt in his purpose. The Liberators and Fortresses had a dual mission. Yes, to destroy targets with bombs. But they were also expected to bait enemy fighters into the air. U.S. fighter support would not engage the enemy unless and until they were busy attacking the bomber formations, assuring our fighters a higher enemy kill ratio. Our fighters would also be free to hit German airfields and ground infrastructure. If the Army Air Forces, in the final evaluation, could not cut off the German supply of airplanes by bombing their factories and hitting their bases, they would defeat them in the long run by simply killing all their experienced fliers.

As the U.S. air armadas began approaching a force of 1,000 bombers, Doolittle was known to openly challenge the Luftwaffe to come up and meet them, and try to do something about it if they could. In a few more months, the balance of power would shift once and for all to the Eighth with the arrival of more abundant and longer range fighter support. But for now, it was an air war of attrition on both sides. This is what the 392nd flew into that wintry March day.

It had been a little over two months since I had made my request for my father's file to Mortuary Affairs in Alexandria, Virginia. I knew from speaking to others who had gone this route that these were the most complete and definitive records of what happened to those killed in action, based on examination of the remains and, when possible, Army investigation and deposition of witnesses. Everything I had done and learned so far was a prologue to receipt of this file.

On the first Tuesday in February 1994, I phoned the Mortuary Affairs office. The woman who answered did not seem the least bit sympathetic to my story. Dryly, she told me to wait while she checked to see if my written request had been received. When she did come back she said, "Yes, we have your letter." Then a silence. "Well, can you give me a definite idea as to when I will hear back from you with the information?" I asked. "No," she answered. Another silence.

I patiently tried again, and for the first time touched on my desire to share information with my family before the March 18, 50th anniversary date. Her response was a long complaint that I had to appreciate what a terrific backlog the department had. She concluded by saying, "There is no routine estimate" for how long a search took and she really couldn't give me the slightest idea when they could send the file. Then she added: "You have to understand we are working on some very important cases."

I took that, bit my tongue, and gave it one more brief shot before hanging up. I knew that the clerk held all the marbles but I refused to concede her any kind of victory. I had taken the moral high ground. I only hoped my appeal would crack the bureaucratic wall.

My compulsion to know what there was to know before the anniversary date was understandable, but mine alone. I tried to force myself to take the longer view. Puzzles would be solved over time, inconsistencies resolved, with persistence and patience. Not on my schedule but on their own.

At the same time I harbored fears. Those with the living memory were passing, fading like the thin paper trail once kept to record their part in history. I knew that the puzzles might simply choose to resist solution. And that, ultimately, all we may say of some of the fallen is that they played their part and paid the price of victory.

My deepest fear, one I would not articulate even to myself, was of atrocity. I did not want my father to have been victimized any more than the fortunes of war and battle ordained. But I had to know. So I continued to try to reach the truth and close the loop of our intertwined lives.

On the last Saturday in February, my son Matt's girlfriend, Renee, was visiting for the weekend. She and Matt had both been undergraduate students at St. Bonaventure University in western New York. Now they had both begun careers, she in Albany and he in Manhattan. I was with them in the kitchen of our house when the mailman delivered a thick package in a brown business envelope. The return address read: Department of the Army, U.S. Total Army Personnel Command - ATTN: TAPC - PED - F, 2461 Eisenhower Ave., Alexandria, VA. *The mortuary records file*. I made my excuses and took the envelope up to my room and locked the door.

The first page was a summary of a forensic examination dated August 9, 1948. It was signed by embalmer George W. Lowry and by the supervising officer, Lt. Jesse C. Harrell. It indicated that my father's skull and jaw had been badly damaged. Bones were missing and all the main ones present were fractured. An extra leg bone in the casket had been removed following established protocol. The document stated that there was no identification tag, but eventually positive identification was made from dental records which were included in the file.

My eyes filled as I read, racing through page after page. There was a seven page report with two pages of attachments, and a related sheaf of papers from the Army Quartermaster's Report of Investigation Area Search. This was done on preprinted forms and seemed to be used for both tanks and aircraft. It was dated May 23, 1946, and signed by Wayne S. Rockwell, 2nd. Lt., 538th QM Group.

This report said an identification tag was present. Date of (original) burial March 22, 1944. Names of others buried in immediate vicinity: seven, was written in, but only the names of Nathan Maylander, Enoch E. Masters, and Leon G. Hancock followed. Name and type of Cemetery: Ettenheimmunster, Civilian Cemetery. Map coordinates and location followed, near Lahr, Baden, Germany. Then the exact location of the single grave with a diagram of the site attached. Line 10: "If grave is marked with cross, give exact markings thereon." The typed response: Rest in Peace. One unknown American Airman killed in action 18 March 1944 in Koecherhof. The source of information: Burgermeister's report. By whom: Burgermeister Tisch. Cause of death: Plane crash. Date of burial: 22 March 1944. How did crash occur: Shot down. So it went.

The summary said that all the remains but one were badly burnt.

Rockwell's hand-drawn topographic map indicated three separate crashes on a mountain above the town. Sites one and two, I knew were the "Sinister Minister" and Cliff Peterson's Lib, "Big Time Operator." They ended up about a football field's length away from each other. The third bomber was pinpointed on the same ridge, about a mile away. To my knowledge, and within the investigative report, it remained unidentified.

The enclosed depositions of local citizens concerning the crash and burial, taken in May 1946, provided a wealth of detail about those events. Both the German and English versions of these documents were included. Each was witnessed and signed under an American officer's supervision.

According to the eyewitnesses, the fires on the mountain above the village burned for the better part of two days. On March 20th, the word spread that the Luftwaffe was removing the bodies from the crash sites. Many of the townspeople went up again to the main site, which had been continuously guarded since the crashes. The villagers gathered on the perimeter, among them the pastor of the local Catholic church and the burgermeister.

Word jumped from the Luftwaffe guards to the people and spread that some of the Americans had been carrying crucifixes and holy pictures, the Madonna and Child. The priest went forward without hesitation and argued with the officials that the Americans deserved a Christian burial. Of course, Nazi policy stated that absolutely no honors should be given to the enemy dead. The burgermeister supported the priest.

The depositions of both men, Theodor Tisch and Father Robert Merkle, summed up these events. According to the priest, "a Catholic funeral for all the American airmen" was held and they were buried in the community cemetery on March 22. A casket was fashioned for each of ten men. "The graves were marked by one big cross with the inscription," which I quoted earlier from Lt.

Rockwell's report. Later, individual crosses were erected on each of the graves. The nuns of the parish pledged to look after the graves.

I knew that my father had been a devout Christian from a family that was religious in the true sense of the word. Dad's oldest brother John was a priest. As I took all of this in, and the tears slowly, unstoppably, rolled out from my eyes, I only wished that my mother and my dad's mother had known these facts for the small comfort they would have represented. In this instance, it seemed, there had been no atrocity, only humanity.

I was surprised by the overwhelming grief that swept over me. My first thought was that it was wrong, selfish. Perhaps I even felt a sense of relief that the burden of not knowing had finally been lifted from me. But I knew it was none of that. I finally realized that as a boy in Brooklyn, and as the young man I had once been, I had never been allowed, or been able to grieve for my father. A man can do that since he has experience and maturity as a reference point. A boy could never grieve for a sense of lost life when he has had no life of his own.

Now, a half century later, the face in the familiar portrait of my father was that of a much younger man than his son was today. I realized that I was now mourning my father in much the way one would mourn the loss of a son, of a life cut too short. And, knowing that, I allowed myself to mourn. For the first time in my life I wept for my father's death. Precious as he was to me, I felt for his pain, his suffering, and the solitary nature of his end.

A final image stuck in my mind of an Army officer kicking at pine needle strewn soil somewhere in the Black Forest. He bends down and, picking up a twig, pokes at the dirt. It was the last two lines of Rockwell's report. "A visit to the scene of the crash revealed very little as the bulk of the planes had been removed. All that could be found was a small piece of canvas and a few globs of molten metal." The remains of a Liberator.

While the 392nd Bomb Group history for the Friedrichshafen mission, compiled in May 1944, ends with the fates of their downed bombers still uncertain, it is possible to continue their story in greater detail based on the later accounts of survivors, German witnesses on the ground, and the 1946 Army site investigation in Ettenheimmunster, Germany.

"Sinister Minister" was afire and almost out of control. The damage done by the flak had been enough to put any hope of a successful return to England in doubt. The fighter attacks had been the clincher. The nose and cockpit were badly damaged and of the officers, all but the bombardier were wounded. As Mike Cugini and Carl Anderson fired the last bursts at departing ME 109s in vain, Covenez called up from the ball turret. The gunners retracted it and then the three of them talked about getting out.

The waist was rapidly filling with smoke. It seemed to be coming from under the wings and belly of #117. Leaning out of the windows, they could see flames on both sides just forward of the wings. Cugini crawled up by the bomb bay and hit the hydraulic lever. As the doors opened up, flames shot all the way up and more black smoke billowed into the waist. He quickly hit the lever again, sealing off the doors. Covenez checked his chute and, without ceremony, jumped out the main hatch. The other two made their preparations.

In the cockpit, Lieutenant Sharpe had stopped arguing with copilot Bandura about who was in better shape to fly the plane. Weakened by shock and the loss of blood from his arm wound, the pilot passed out. Sergeant Wallace had hurriedly cleaned up Sharpe's arm and shoulder and then did the best he could with Bandura's knee and upper leg, which were also full of shrapnel.

Wallace stood by while Norb Bandura tried to level the Lib from a long flat dive.

In the nose, bombardier Richardson sat behind his turret guns and told Bandura on the interphone that they should all get out. Behind him, on the floor of the navigator's work area, Lieutenant McGuire lay unconscious, his bleeding head propped awkwardly against the cabin wall.

Cugini didn't have his chute on and ran to where he should have left it. He struggled to get into the harness and secure it. Then he realized he didn't have his boots on, only the felt slippers they sometimes wore aboard. He ran back and forth frantically but couldn't find his shoes. Glancing out the open hatch, he saw that they were getting much too close to the ground. He jumped. Anderson was only seconds behind him. He took a last look at the tail, but Maylander hadn't budged for a long time. He let himself drop out.

The ship fell into a steeper dive that rapidly brought it closer to the side of a forested mountain. Bandura and Wallace knew it was too late. Richardson glanced at McGuire and thought he was gone, as the bombardier stumbled to the nose wheel doors and released them.

The blast of cold air blowing into the nose from the opening brought the Navigator back to consciousness. He felt the terrible numbness in his head and the side of his face. He seemed to have little control over his body but instinctively knew the plane was about to crash and tried to feel his way toward the nose wheel exit. Tremendous centrifugal force pressed him against the cabin wall as he desperately inched his way. "Sweet Jesus," he said. "Help us."

Floating down, Lt. Cliff Peterson saw his ship, #981, drop past his chute and crash, seconds before he crunched to the ground. He was struggling with his shrouds, with part of his chute wrapped in a tree, when Sgt. Hinshaw found him. Hinshaw could see that the wounded Peterson was in shock, but he knew they both had to find some cover quickly. There were patches of snow and bare ground, and Malcolm tried to lead the Lieutenant around the snowy places so their trail would be harder to follow. Just over a rise, about 200 yards from where they had landed, they heard the ammo go on their "Big Time Operator" and saw the smoke shoot up.

Cugini too, saw smoke and fire up over the tree tops as he gathered in his chute. He was standing in six inches of wet snow and the felt slippers were dissolving under his feet. It was cold. He heard rounds exploding from the ship in the distance and his impulse was to go there to help. At the same time he realized it was impossible, that it was a certain way to be captured or killed.

In the village, schoolboy Herbert Griesbaum saw the smoke rising from the wreck sites up on the mountain and felt both pride and a sense of righteous revenge in his young breast. He knew the destruction those bombers would bring when they had first passed overhead. Only minutes before he had watched as the formation of dots high up in the blue was attacked by what seemed to be a single German ME 109. Then he, and dozens like him, had cheered at the three falling American planes. No others from the American formation had helped them as they were being engaged by the Messerschmitt. Rather, they just kept flying west as if nothing had happened. They were anything but brave, he thought.

The next day, Sunday, he and his friends would go up and see what they had done to the Americans.

Crossing the road between the church and the parish house, next to town hall, Pastor Merkle looked up at the smoke on the mountain and said a prayer for the repose of the mortal souls of these war dead.

Herbert's school teacher Valentin Strickfaden was on the mountain during the ME 109's daring attack on the bombers. He saw them crash. Two came very close. He had seen men parachuting as the ship closest to him fell. Both planes exploded and many little explosions followed. It would not be wise to get too close.

Suddenly, an airman came down a short distance from Valentin in an open plateau on the hill. The teacher ran to him and helped him remove the parachute. The American lay there on the ground and when Valentin started to help him up, the flier showed him his wounded knee. There was a hut or lean-to there, on the edge of the field where the Koecherhof settlement had once been. The teacher made a crutch for the airman and, placing his arm around his own shoulder, helped him to the shelter.

Valentin fashioned a rough splint for the airman. While applying it to his leg, he heard someone crying out for help. The school teacher followed the sounds to a badly wounded American officer lying on the ground. His whole right side, arm, ribs, and leg seemed broken. Strickfaden half carried, half dragged him to the hut and then brought snow to cool the wounds of both the Americans.

Valentin learned their names. The first one he had found was called Rosko. The officer was named Russell Vreiling. Then a third American entered the shack. Waist gunner Carl Anderson was unhurt from his fall from the "Sinister Minister". He immediately set to helping the German care for his fellow fliers. He used his morphine to bring Vreiling some relief. The teacher produced some wine and they all sat there, behind enemy lines, just four men at the end of a crazy day of destruction and resurrection sharing a few slugs of Deutschland vino. They soon heard the civilian patrol coming.

Hinshaw had peeked over the rise and seen the rest of the crew taken into custody below. He told Cliff Peterson. They took some water from a stream and Cliff took stock of himself. He hurt all over from shrapnel wounds. He didn't know it but there was a chunk in the middle of his eye. The sleeve of his electrically heated flying suit was gone and the wires hung out crazily. He slowly took off his leather flying gloves. Underneath, the silk liners were soaked with blood. Within hours, both men would become POWs.

The search party arriving at the hut included various volunteers from Ettenheim and nearby Lahr. They fashioned a makeshift stretcher for Vreiling and they all marched down the road. One of the officials stopped at a house and brought out a car, and they shuffled Anderson and Rosko into it for the drive to the town hall down the mountain in Ettenheimmunster.

Valentin Strickfaden and the farmer Griesbaum carried Russ Vreiling all the way down to town. That night, when he was alone, Strickfaden took out the silk glove that Vreiling had given him. It had been an odd gesture that struck the teacher as chivalrous in a fashion. He unfolded the little scrap of paper, on which the three had each written their names, and smoothed it out. He sat there, saying each name aloud, and wondered if he sounded American.

The scene on the mountain was repeated that afternoon all over southwestern Germany and into the occupied French side of the Rhine, not always with such benign results. As Del Johnson came to ground, he tried to put most of the force of the landing onto his uninjured right leg and then rolled back into the snow. A group of townspeople immediately walked over to him like they had been waiting to enter from stage left. Two of them won his particular attention. There was a young man, no more than sixteen, in full black uniform, carrying a military rifle. The older man, probably a cobbler, was wearing a full length leather apron. The cobbler frisked him down, repeating something that sounded like "pistolah?" Johnson shook his head and said, "No." His hands fell on Del's good new pocket knife and the American automatically started to pull it back. The kid in the black outfit then stepped back, swung the gun down and, cocking it, shoved the barrel into Del's gut. Johnson said goodbye to his favorite pocket knife.

James Ross, the Scot aboard "The Jungle Princess," went out the camera hatch when he heard the horn. They were only at 10,000 feet when he pulled the rip cord. When it came all the way out in his hand, he thought that he had broken it, not knowing it was supposed to come out. He had his G. I. shoes tied to the chute harness. As the chute ripped open, a shoe caught under the strap and kicked against his side so hard that it broke a rib. The pain made him nauseous as he fell.

Working his chute to avoid a high tension wire and an oncoming train, he landed at a crazy angle in a field, breaking his leg in two places. He was met by a Free Frenchman, who flashed his hidden credential, a pin on the underside of his lapel. But seeing what a sorry state Ross was in, the Frenchman could do nothing but pretend to willingly turn him in to the Germans. The Scot was in no condition to make an escape.

Chester Strickler, sole survivor of the Books crew, "Old Glory," landed standing up in a field near Hardt, not far from where the plane crashed. An elderly man carrying an old rifle and a little redheaded boy approached him. The little fellow spoke good English and looking up at him said, "American airman …do you have chewing gum?" Chester nodded and began to reach into his jacket. The old man immediately raised and fired from 10 yards into the American's chest. Strickler stared at him in disbelief. He had already been banged around so much that he felt more shock than pain. He would recover in a German hospital over the next five months.

The Army investigative report of the Ettenheimmunster crash sites and burials contained individual depositions of the local German principals. Closely examining these as well as more contemporary additional evidence permits a step-by-step reconstruction of the final disposition of the remains of the American crewmen from the viewpoint of ordinary citizens. While this description covers some ground outlined earlier in the Rockwell summary report of June 1946, it presents a much more complete picture of what actually happened.

After the fires cooled, the wrecks remained too hot and too much of a risk for a time. But on Monday, March 20, more Wermacht and Luftwaffe personnel arrived at the scene and the investigative work began in earnest. Many townspeople were lured up the mountain by the news of this operation, including Father Merkle and Burgermeister Theodor Tisch.

Tisch was given I.D. tags for two of the dead at the higher site. The Luftwaffe people from Freiburg pointed out another two bodies and casually gave him the names. The Luftwaffe took all the personal effects into their possession. The burgermeister spoke to the undertaker, Friedrich Joos, about coffins for the eleven men who now lay in rows under the wings of the planes. There were four at the high site and seven at the lower.

The priest heard villagers repeating what some of the guards had said, that the airmen had holy pictures, medals, crucifixes among their personal possessions. The priest engaged Tisch and the military officials, arguing that these men were obviously Catholic, though he suspected this was not entirely true. Father Merkle said the Americans deserved a solemn Christian burial. Without hesitation the burgermeister joined the argument. Tisch, who had fought in the first World War, said: "These men were soldiers.

They deserve our respect." The Luftwaffe acceded to the civil authorities' request. Of the eleven dead at the two sites, one at the lower location on the mountain was not burned as all the others had been. This corpse, a man of dark curly hair and average build, was removed by the Luftwaffe for separate burial at Lahr. No explanation was offered.

By the early afternoon, the soldiers had removed the bodies and anything of military or intelligence value from the wrecks. Salvage would be handled later for these two sites and another some distance off. The dead from this third plane, some six or seven, were also shipped to Lahr for burial under Luftwaffe supervision. For the moment, there were no military guards at the crash scenes, where people from the town were still picking over the wreckage of the two Liberators.

Herbert Griesbaum and his friends climbed up the mountain on foot as soon as school got out. With him were his regular chums, Kreig, Adams, Raiff Jager and Werner Nicklas. The boys swarmed over the wrecks, taking turns pivoting a machine gun that was still in its mount. Werner had brought his box camera to record the event. Going down the hill toward home, Herbert realized he probably hadn't gotten into the pictures and pressed Werner to take another at the second site in the woods. High up on the fuselage, young Nicklas caught him laughing triumphantly. In the background, on the tail, were the numbers 100117. It was an adventure they would remember.

All was not ready until Wednesday, March 22, when a slow file of priests and acolytes, carrying processional crucifix and candles, made its way from the church up the hill to the new communal cemetery. Several officials, including the local Nazi leader, and some townspeople, gathered there for a truly unique event and certainly one of the largest mass burials in the history of this little village on the edge of the Black Forest. The burgermeister's grandson was so impressed that he had brought his camera.

Undertaker Friedrich Joos and gravedigger Georg Gassman had done a good job creating a trench across row five in plot one of the pristine little cemetery. Now they struggled to get each of the ten caskets into the earth, while the priests intoned prayers and blessings in Latin and sprinkled holy water on the wooden boxes. "May Thy perpetual light shine upon them. May they and all the souls of the faithful departed rest in peace," Merkle called out in a firm voice.

All the snow was gone. Green shoots were beginning to push up from the dank cold soil. There was the promise of spring, but that meant very little in 1944. The ceremony was over. Women put their rosaries away and men covered their heads once again. And they left the Liberators under a big white wooden cross that said who they had been.

On July 31, they found the "Big Time Operator" waist gunner Enoch Masters in the woods of Neuwald Fohrenbuhl. He was wrapped in what remained of his chute and his skull was stoved in. No personal effects. They buried him in the same row with the other men of the 392nd.

Daybreak on March 18, 1994, came up bright, clear, and crisp. The McGuires, all six of us, arose and somehow managed to get out the door together on time, looking respectable and acting with a fair amount of civility toward one another. There were patches of snow on the ground as we walked around the street to 6:45 a.m. mass at St. Augustine's Church.

This was not our routine practice on Friday mornings or any morning, particularly the day after St. Patrick's Day. So the

Navigator's son was a little proud of them for being with me to hear my father's name read as one of the intentions of the mass, and to pray for him. The celebrant was Father Joe De Santo, whom we all held in high regard. The priest spoke briefly of Lieutenant McGuire, of his death fifty years earlier and of the men who had served and died with him. He spoke of their spirits converging around the altar at the moment of consecration. I, the father of this family, was strongly moved by his simple words.

Besides us, there were no more than seven or eight faithful early risers in the church. But for me, it was a mass our family would hold in our hearts all the days of our lives. Afterward, we all went our separate ways. To the routine. TGIF.

That night, I was alone in the kitchen at home when Uncle Gerry and Aunt Marilyn called. My dad's baby brother explained that they were on two different extensions so they could conference call in a way.

Gerry said that they didn't want the day to end without letting me know that they were thinking of me and my dad on this fiftieth anniversary of his death. We had a long, funny, sad talk, full of memories and anecdotes of the kind of man Bill Senior had been. It was in a way an Irish wake and about as good as they get. When I hung up, I was happier, and grateful to them for both remembering and for reaching out to me.

On March 22, I ended up in the hospital for a few days because of some blips in my heart and pain in one arm and shoulder. The doctors never really found out what the problem was but the tests discovered some arteriosclerosis. I suppose you could call it hardening of the arteries in the area of my heart. It did set me to thinking a little less about my father's mortality and a little more about my own.

Our good friends for thirty years, Ginny and Bill Gilfillan, had rented a beach house at Nags Head, North Carolina, the next week and invited us to be their guests. Ginny called me in the hospital that Thursday night and told me, in no uncertain terms, that if I messed up the trip she would personally make me pay for the rest of my life. I laughed, but knowing Ginny, I believed her too.

With my wife and I prevailing on the physicians with various soap opera tales, and reassuring them that Ginny was a nurse and that I would be sure to take all my medications, I was released Friday afternoon.

Sunday morning I was walking beaches on the Outer Banks, the best therapy a man could ask for in any season. The temperature was in the 60s but a stiff wind blew and the beach was a mess, the surf tremendous from the last remnants of still another northeaster. The sand blew in a constant sheet three to four feet above the ground. It was a seaside version of *Lawrence of Arabia.*

My eyes took in the more interesting shells and stones as I walked along the packed wet sand at the surf's edge. I stopped to pick up a broken piece of shell worn smooth by the action of sand and water. There was an eyelike opening in the upper quadrant. I realized why it had caught my attention then. It was a natural copy in miniature of the mask in the musical *Phantom of the Opera.*

As I walked and felt the cool smoothness of the shell, it reminded me of a speech I had once written for the millionairess head of a fund-raising ball and summer concert. Wearing masks at Mardi Gras, festivals, and carnivals in the time of the late Middle Ages was not done so much to hide one's identity or to frighten or surprise. Rather, it was intended to remind all, including the mask wearer, that this individual was more than what we routinely saw and knew. "The me you know is not all of me. I have other dimensions and potentials of which you know nothing," the mask wearer said. "I have a soul." This is the heart of the meaning of all types of Day of the Dead rituals. On the beach, I remembered these old words of mine as I pocketed the shell.

It was quite a week. We sunbathed, walked, and explored. We ate and drank up a storm, mostly in the house's big kitchen and on its enormous oceanfront deck.

On Holy Thursday night, the four of us went out to a French country-style restaurant to celebrate my birthday, which was the next day. Then we watched a video of *Moonstruck* with the other house guests, Ginny and Bill's two daughters, a boyfriend, a niece and her husband. Except for daughter Kate, age ten, they were all in their twenties. After the film, we went out on the deck to face the elements, reinforced by nightcaps, many nightcaps. With the kids, we bayed at the moon and took in the endless tapestry of the stars. And we all sang several choruses of *"That's Amore,"* poorly, but loudly.

Sometime after midnight I saw two shooting stars cross paths. First one then the other, right under my nose. Then I swore a low star was reflecting light on the water. Ginny swore I was drunk. In any event, we all agreed, Billy McGuire was fifty-one years old! It was Good Friday, April 1, 1994.

On the third of June, my whole family drove up to Saratoga Springs, New York, for our son Matt's wedding to his dear Renee the next day. It was a perfectly glorious weekend and wedding. Our daughter Julianna would be wed on the 25th. I picked the weekend of the 10th to go up to Buffalo and visit Mike and Arlene Cugini. "It's something I just have to do," I told my wife, after having postponed the trip twice earlier in the year. It was a busy time in our lives, but Bernadette understood.

The long train ride from Pennsylvania Station got me in to Buffalo about twenty minutes late. The Cuginis were waiting for me as I stepped off onto the platform. I actually recognized Mike from the photograph of the crew fifty years earlier. He was a slim, almost slight man with long arms, who had changed little. At 5'10", he was about three inches shorter than me.

They both gave me a warm reception and took me out to dinner at their favorite local tavern. Another couple, friends of the Cuginis since high school, came over to the table and Mike proudly introduced me to them.

After dinner we sat in the Cugini living room together and talked, while I took notes and looked through Mike's World War II scrapbook. There was the picture once again, and he identified each of the members of the #117 crew for me.

The old airman talked about their training and the trip back to New York in October 1943 for their transatlantic crossing on the *Queen Mary* or *Queen Elizabeth*, he wasn't sure which one.

We went over his accounting of what had happened on March 18, 1944, one more time and resolved some details that had seemed apparent contradictions to me from our earlier phone conversations: "Communications had gone out," but he then referred to the voices on the interphone. Now, he explained that radio communications with England and the rest of the formation had quit, but the shipboard system kept working till the end. In the original telling he thought he had parachuted some fifteen miles from the crash site. This time, he spoke of seeing the flames from the impact site over the trees.

We watched the end of the Knicks playoff game together and had one more beer. We spoke of Mike's beloved Buffalo Bills football team and how they might fare in the fall. I had offered to stay in a local hotel but they insisted on my spending the night, and made me comfortable in an upstairs bedroom.

The next day Arlene made bacon and eggs at Mike's request and then he drove me around the old neighborhood where he had grown up and spent all his life. He and his wife had run a luncheonette-style restaurant called John and Mary's, and then one called Mickey's for many years. He showed me the McDonald's where all the old guys would get together each morning for coffee. There were fewer and fewer of them left, he admitted sadly.

The Cuginis had dabbled in the travel business as well, and Mike continued to be involved. He and Arlene loved to gamble and make trips to Atlantic City and other gambling spots. Each day he played the same three digit number in the New York lottery. I learned that the couple had a daughter on Long Island and a son and granddaughter out west.

We stopped at a car dealership that was having an antique auto show. The exhibit featured about twelve cars and trucks from the 1920s, all in great shape. It was still before 9 a.m., and whoever was supposed to be watching the store must have gone out for coffee. We were the only two people on the property. Mike and I examined the first Ford pickup truck and Cugini, from behind the wheel, admitted that he had tinkered around with one during the Depression.

We drove past his old school, Kensington High, and Mike spoke of what a wonderful community Cheektowaga had been. But it changed after the war, particularly in the 1960s, he said, and not for the better. At midday, I threw my note pad and the few things I had into my one small bag, and the three of us drove back to the train station.

It was a perfect early spring day, and the Cuginis spoke of the gardening they would do later that afternoon. At the station, they told me to check at the window to make sure the train was on time; it often ran late. They waited for me in the car. They were right, it was a half-hour behind schedule. But I lied so they could be on their way.

As they got out of the car to say goodbye, I thanked them profusely for their gracious and wonderful hospitality. Mike put both hands on my shoulders and looking into my eyes said, "I hope I have made a friend."

I answered, "Of course," and hugging him said, "Friends for life." I kissed Arlene goodbye and watched them pull away.

I waited on the platform. Spring flowers and weeds grew along the tracks, gently moving in a light breeze. A freight train lumbered by, and I compulsively counted 109 boxcars. Then again, the only sound was bees buzzing among the blossoms.

On the long trip down the length of New York alongside the old Erie Canal system, I thought of my hosts and of what I had asked and what I had failed or forgotten to ask. I took consolation in the thought that Mike could now be a regular checkpoint and reference source as I continued to try to unravel the final details of the Friedrichshafen mission. I got home in time to see the last ten minutes of the Rangers Stanley Cup win. They wrapped it up that Tuesday evening and the championship was finally theirs. Fifty-four years of ice hockey frustration came to an end. In the jubilant arena, one sign held by a grinning spectator read: "Now I can die in peace."

My company, Seabury & Smith, part of a big insurance and consulting firm, had involved employees in doing some fund raising for the New York City Ronald McDonald House, a place for children under treatment for cancer to stay with their families at little or no cost to them. The employees arranged a raffle with a first prize of round trip tickets for two to England or Scotland on British Airways. I invested $10 and kept my fingers crossed.

The day of the drawing, the office also arranged for a night at Shea Stadium for a Mets baseball game and a barbecue dinner for some of the McDonald House children and their parents or escorts. I was supposed to go. That day, July 14, was Bastille Day, and I met my high-powered, wisecracking P.R. man friend Brian Martin for a glass of wine and Le Hamburger at the counter of the Brasserie Restaurant.

I got back to the office about 2:05, just in time to see everyone gathered in one corner for the McDonald's drawing. About a hundred people. A young lady reached in to the pile of ticket stubs and they read my name. I made my way to the front and shook hands all around. Turning to the group, I said: "Fifty years ago this past March, my father was killed in a bomber raid over Germany. What winning this will allow me to do is to go over to England and visit his old base and cross the Channel to see where he is buried in France for the first time. Thank you for helping make it possible."

With that, I noticed a few teary eyes out among the audience. Later, a young man came up to me and said, "You know, I have never seen a group of people who were so happy not to win something until today."

It rained at the ballpark that night. I met the Mets' Mookie Wilson in the left field skybox where the McDonald's dinner was held. The game was delayed. I spoke with two guests from British Air about the trip. I had up to a year to use the tickets. They said they could bump me up to business class if I was flexible about when I went. The rain grew heavier in the bright ballpark lights, puddling in the tarps. The game was canceled. It was a season the Mets should have canceled as well.

Earlier that same day, Arlene Cugini wrote me a letter that through mishandling, I would not receive for several weeks:

Dear Bill,

This is very difficult to pass on to you. I lost my Michael June 22. I came home from work and found him dead, in the process of getting dressed. He was fine when I left for work, but as we talked about it, he had a serious heart problem. God bless him, he didn't suffer. It was a pleasure meeting you briefly. Will keep in touch.

Sincerely and fondly,
Arlene Cugini

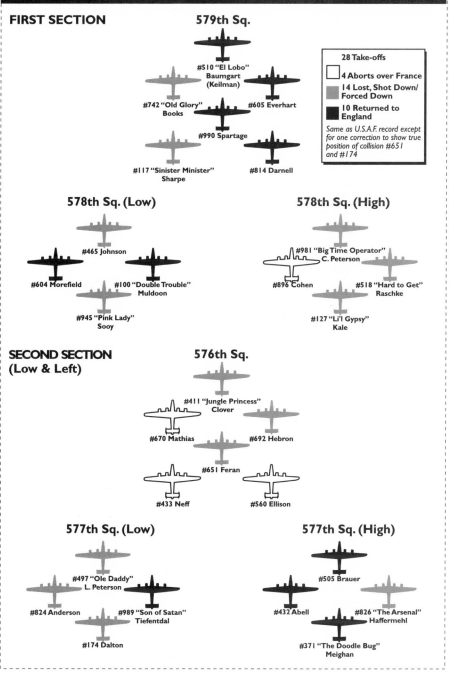

392nd BOMB GROUP FORMATION, 3/18/44

FIRST SECTION

579th Sq.

#510 "El Lobo" Baumgart (Keilman)

#742 "Old Glory" Books

#605 Everhart

#990 Spartage

#117 "Sinister Minister" Sharpe

#814 Darnell

28 Take-offs

☐ 4 Aborts over France

▨ 14 Lost, Shot Down/ Forced Down

■ 10 Returned to England

Same as U.S.A.F. record except for one correction to show true position of collision #651 and #174

578th Sq. (Low)

#465 Johnson

#604 Morefield

#100 "Double Trouble" Muldoon

#945 "Pink Lady" Sooy

578th Sq. (High)

#981 "Big Time Operator" C. Peterson

#896 Cohen

#518 "Hard to Get" Raschke

#127 "Li'l Gypsy" Kale

SECOND SECTION (Low & Left)

576th Sq.

#411 "Jungle Princess" Clover

#670 Mathias

#692 Hebron

#651 Feran

#433 Neff

#560 Ellison

577th Sq. (Low)

#497 "Ole Daddy" L. Peterson

#824 Anderson

#989 "Son of Satan" Tiefentdal

#174 Dalton

577th Sq. (High)

#505 Brauer

#432 Abell

#826 "The Arsenal" Haffermehl

#371 "The Doodle Bug" Meighan

The approximate route of the 392nd BG for its attack on Friedrichshafen, Germany, 3.18.1944. A 360 degrees climbing turn over the English Channel may have contributed to a delay in reaching the target and, consequently, to the loss of fighter air cover for the group.

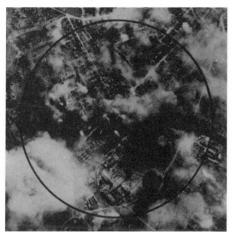

Bombardier's view of Friedrichshafen targets, showing bomb impact smoke as well as some thin cloud cover. 3.18.44. (Photo: J. Marsteller)

42100117, "Sinister Minister," taking off at Wendling, England. (Photo: 392nd Archive)

392nd Liberators taxi for take off alongside the mud at Wendling, winter 1943-44. (Photo: C. Peterson)

American airmen at Wendling tensely await the return of their planes. (Photo: A. Enlow)

Friedrichshafen target and Lake Constance as seen from the 392nd BG attack force at approximately 20,000 ft. altitude, 3.18.44. (Photo: J. Marsteller)

Wendling Liberators taxi toward take off in 1944. (Photo: E. Barber, 392nd Archive)

Wendling ground crew personnel load Liberators with 500 pounders and small cluster bombs in 1944. (Photo: O. Mackey and E. Barber, 392nd Archive)

"Double Trouble," 578th Sq. Liberator which made it back from Friedrichshafen, in 1943-44. (Photo: E. Barber, 392nd Archive)

Part of the crew of the "Sinister Minister," #117, posed in front of a B17 at a base in the southwestern U.S., Summer 1943. (L-R) Rear: Bill McGuire, navigator; Mike Cugini, waist gun; Frank Wallace, radio; Bill McGowan, ball turret. Front: Frank Richardson, bombardier; Bill Sharpe, pilot; Ralph Huffman, engineer; Carl Anderson, waist gun. Missing from photo: Norbert Bandura, copilot; Nathan Maylander, tail gun; Clarence Covenez, substitute ball turret. Covenez, Anderson, and Cugini survived. 3.18.44.

The "Big Time Operator," #981, crew: (L-R) Rear: Jimmie C. Byrd, tail gun; Ora Harrell, ball turret; Hugh M. Hinshaw, engineer; Enoch Masters, waist gun; Leon G. Hancock, waist gun; Eugene Rosko, radio; Front: Edmund J. Brown, bombardier; Russ J. Vreiling, copilot; Cliff Peterson, pilot; C.L. Fremstead, navigator (did not fly 3.18.44). Peterson, Vreiling, Hinshaw, Rosko, and the replacement navigator survived. (Photo: H. M. Hinshaw)

The 390th BG B17, #925, crew: (L-R) F. Grover Wallace, waist gun; Theodore P. Aycock, bombardier; Loyd G. Breedlove, copilot; Dominick M. Robbe, ball turret; C.C. Marshall, navigator; Harry M. Houck, radio/gunner; Robert W. Biesecker, pilot; Peter Repka, engineer; Wm. E. Rooks, tail gun; Michael J. Farrowich, waist gun. Houck, Wallace, and Farrowich survived the 3.18.44 mission. (Photo: H. Houck)

"Glad to see ya, Little Friend!" A Republic P47 Thunderbolt escort, as seen from a B24. (Photo: J. Marsteller)

The B17's regular navigator, C.C. Marshall (far right), took on a new assignment just prior to the March 18 mission and survived the war. Pilot Biesecker and bombardier Aycock, along with five crew members, were killed. (Photo: H. Houck)

392nd BG Liberators encounter German flak barrage. (Photo: J. Marsteller)

392nd BG B24s in formation. (Photo: J. Marsteller)

B24 navigator at his cramped workstation beneath celestial observation bubble. (Photo: G. Hatton)

392nd BG formation under flak bombardment, as seen from another Liberator. (Photo: E. Barber, 392nd Archive)

Wendling B24s, with silver finish and new markings, drop bombs on target. Second half of 1944. (Photo: J. Marsteller, 392nd Archive)

Two 392nd BG Liberators over farmland, December 1943. (Photo: J. Marsteller, 392nd Archive)

Two Wendling Liberators, black, against a sea of snow white cloud cover. (Photo: J. Marsteller)

BELOW: Schoolboy Herbert Griesbaum atop the wreckage of J100117, "Sinister Minister."

ABOVE: Lt. Dallas O. Books' Liberator wreckage, 3.18.44: tail section, "Steinreute," Hardt, Germany. Photo taken 3.19.1944. (Photo: Archive Carsten Kohlmann)

A Luftwaffe flak guard stands watch over the wrecked cockpit of the Books' Liberator, near Hardt. Only one airman survived. (Photo: J. Marsteller)

Citizens of Mariazell, Germany, look over wreckage of Lt. Rex Johnson's Liberator on Sunday, 3.19.1944. (Photo: J. Marsteller)

Wreckage of Lt. Rex Johnson's Liberator, following the Friedrichshafen mission, draws the curiosity of the citizens of Mariazell. (Photo: J. Marsteller)

Caskets and the burial ceremony of the American airmen who fell in enemy territory, 3.22.1944, Ettenheimmunster. Pastor Merkle of St. Landelin Church, in the Roman collar, holds open prayer book while being assisted, on his left, by his deacon.

The Church of St. Landelin, Ettenheimmunster, Germany, today. It is virtually unchanged since the 18th century. (Photo: ©Kurt Gramer, D74321 Bietigheim-Bissengen)

Baseball Coach McGuire (center-suit), with his young Our Lady of Perpetual Help (OLPH) charges in the mid-1930s. The little tow-headed mascot, seated front right, is believed to be Bill's younger brother, Gerry McGuire.

An official pose for the camera, and waiting for a rebound (dark shirt, #7), Bill Sr. played three years of varsity basketball at Brooklyn College and captained the team in his senior year, 1937-38.

The OLPH parish basketball team, 1939-40. Bill McGuire is second from the left, standing.

Wedding smiles contrasted with stormy weather as Bill and Micky began married life, February 1942.

BELOW: The author's parents, Bill and Muriel or Micky. 2nd Lt. McGuire wears his navigator's wings.

The author (center) with Wendling airfield guides, Denis Duffield, left, and Derek Patfield, at the Ploughshare, Beeston, England, June 1995.

ABOVE: The author and his wife, Bernadette, at the Wendling, England 392nd BG Memorial obelisk, June 1995.

LEFT: The author at his father's grave, Lorraine American Cemetery, near St. Avold, France, Father's Day, 1995.

Colonel Myron Keilman in the early 1990s at a reunion. As a Major he headed up the 579th Squadron of the 392nd BG, and was the group leader on the 3.18.1944 mission. He passed away in 1998. (Photo: J. Marsteller)

The author (center), with Jim Morris (left) and Jim Marsteller, cousins and fellow researchers, National Archive II, College Park, Maryland, March 1996. (Photo: J. Morris)

From January 1943 until June 1944, the 392nd BG was commanded by Col. Irvine Rendle, and the Wendling airmen were known as "Rendle's Raiders." Here Col. Rendle (L) pins the Air Medal on Lt. Cliff Peterson at Wendling. (Photo: C. Peterson)

Bill McGuire, Jr., the author, with Cliff Peterson, May 1996, Winter Park, Florida.

The B24 "All American," Labor Day weekend, 1995, Floyd Bennett Field, Brooklyn, NY. This is the same ship the author later flew in with his own son, Bill McGuire III.

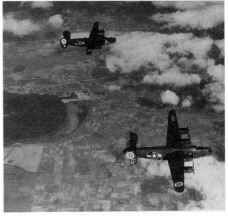

Ettenheimmunster's Town Hall, as it looks today, held the American POWs the evening of 3.18.1944 before they were passed into the hands of the Luftwaffe. Magistrate Franz Josef Helle had his office here in 1995. (above left)

The row of graves, as it looks today, was the burial site of the American airmen at Ettenheimmunster, New Cemetery, Germany. (below left)

Two 392nd BG Liberators on a mission, 1943-44.(Photo: E. Barber, 392nd Archive)

The facade of the Memorial Chapel, Lorraine American Cemetery, St. Avold, France, where the figure of St. Avold blesses the rows of white monuments. (left)

Gold and silver bust of St. Landelin, legendary martyr of Ettenheimmunster. The medallion depicts his severed head. (Photo: Foto Oehler-Ettenheim) (above)

The Ettenheimmunster Benedictine monastery as it looked in its heyday. It lasted more than a thousand years, well into the 19th century. Three American heavy bombers crashed on the small mountain behind the monastery on 3.18.1944.

LEFT: 2nd Lt. McGuire, after completing his training as a navigator, summer 1943.

BELOW: Mother and son, Muriel and Billy McGuire, about 1944.

BELOW: The author and the rest of the McGuire "crew" about 1990: Molly Ann, Bill, Bernadette, Matthew, and Julianna. (Photo: N. Manion)

Book III
Father's Day/Among the Witnesses

I imagine an amateur shrink or experienced TV soap watcher might attribute my sudden bout of dedicated interest in my father's history to a form of male menopause or mid-life crisis. I certainly had my share of '90s style corporate stress, money problems, and family complications. But no more so than a good segment of John Q. Public. In any event, I had become caught up in the step-by-step progression that was unfolding before me. And now, I was going to Europe to see the places that had been the focus of so much of my recent attention. Self-analysis was the furthest thing from my mind. "You're on a mission," one of my friends said to me with real admiration. And dammit, he was right.

Mike's death, sad as it was, did not dampen my enthusiasm for what was to come. Just the opposite. Now I had the added sense that he too was pulling for me to get to where I had to go.

That summer and fall, however, was a time of abrupt transition in our lives, so much so that the prospect of Europe almost receded from our anticipation. We had sold our house of twenty plus years and taken an attractive apartment in our town. The children were almost gone from our lives in an immediate day-to-day sense. Only young Molly remained with us. The oldest, Bill or "Stretch," had finally shipped out reluctantly. But I missed our 6'7" gentle giant. Daughter Julianna, who always kept us laughing, and brother Matt had spouses and places of their own now. Matt was always our own built-in cruise line recreation director and cheerleader: "Well, what are we gonna do next?" was his favorite question, as he'd clap his hands together in expectation. Molly missed them all.

What kind of kids were they? Take Matt, for example. In 1989, I was in a period of protracted unemployment after being let go by the bank that I had worked for over their marketing policy. I had to tell him then, in Matt's sophomore year of college, that I didn't see how it was possible for him to continue in school for the next semester. The money just wasn't there. Matt paid attention, frowning, asking the right questions. Then resolved, his mood changed. And he told me not to worry about it, that we would find a way the semester after that to get on track, and he would work to earn some money to help.

Our conversation at an end, he headed for the door. In relief and admiration I told him, "You know, I like your spirit." With one hand on the doorknob, Matthew turned and smiling at his father said, "Well, who do you think I get it from?"

Europe would be expensive too. The original idea for the office raffle was to pick up hotel costs in England for the winner, as well as the airfare. Despite every effort however, the best the office could manage was the air tickets. But, by hook or by crook, I was convinced that going now was the right thing to do.

Bernadette and I had never been to Europe, "Never been east of Montauk and Bar Harbor," I used to say. We had been too busy raising a family to join the jetsetting age. The raffle windfall was my one sure way to get to my father's grave though, and I would take it. We spent the winter buying travel books, rail tickets, studying accommodation options and trying to strike a balance between a well-planned trip and the flexibility to allow for some uncertainties along the way.

The events of fifty years ago were much in the news, beginning with the anniversary of D-Day the Monday after Matt's wedding. I was personally struck by how the magnificent courage, dedication, and dignity of the participating Normandy veterans we saw on television had turned the cardboard hype of the media on its collective ear and simply galvanized the nation, in awe. This was something authentic, and authenticity of any import usually reduces the commentators to babbling and long silent pauses. It was one glorious reality check and a certain reminder of our precious heritage.

A parade was planned for New York City in the fall of 1995 to celebrate the vets and the anniversary of the end of WWII. It was to be a national parade. I read a letter-to-the-editor of the *New York Post* criticizing the parade idea. The letter also attacked an earlier *Post* editorial supporting the parade plan. The letter said it was all a glorification of war. In response, I fired off a letter of my own and the newspaper published it on March 31, on the eve of my fifty-second birthday. "What the WWII Parade Is Really About," the headline read. It was a long letter, but I will quote part of it here because it says something about my mindset in the months before my trip to Europe.

> *Thanks largely to the power of the naysayers, it seems there is little left anymore to celebrate in community, as a people. But the battle-hardened joy felt in 1945 withstands the test of time, as we saw so clearly in Normandy last June. Once again it would beckon us together, on our own shores, in our own city. So I for one will be there to salute the veteran septuagenarians and the conscience and valor they stand for. And I will be arm-and-arm with as many of my children as I can collar. If there are prayers mixed with the cheers that never again will we have to make such sacrifices, so much the better. The people who will be marching, and the people who will be cheering them know the habit of prayer as well as any.*

In the early spring we christened our first grandchild, darling Lily, born to our daughter Julianna and her husband, Peter DiPaola. She was a beautiful, happy little baby who suddenly occupied a big part of the lives of both my wife and me. We would miss her during the two weeks we planned to be away.

One night that early May, coming home to Westchester on the train from Manhattan, I noticed an ad in the lower right corner of a page in my evening newspaper. "Remember The Veterans on the 50th Anniversary of VE Day, May 8," the ad read. It was framed in a ribbon festooned box with an American eagle at the base. It continued:

In memory of the person you know who lost their life during WWII, place a VE Day commemorative in memoriam in Gannett Suburban Newspapers on Monday, May 8 for all to see. It's a wonderful way to have your loved one remembered and it makes for a lasting keepsake in the years to come.

I wasn't too sure about that, but I didn't like the idea of just forgetting about this special issue of the newspaper either. The McGuires hailed from Brooklyn. No one in the upper reaches of New York would probably have known my father. On the other hand I thought that what I had learned about my dad and the planned trip by a local resident was a good story in keeping with the remembrances and bringing the past back into the present.

I called the paper and learned that a whole section of articles about people's connections to the European war was planned but it already was closed out. However, one person put me in touch with another and after four conversations an interview was arranged.

The newspaper sent a reporter and photographer to the apartment and I told my story. That Monday, the paper led off its special commemorative on page one and right there was a teaser for my story on page two. There it was, with even the photo of my solemn chubby face. As a public relations man, I knew as well as any how publicity was a two-edged sword, but this was all positive and true. I couldn't have done it better myself, and in times to come the article served as a neat summary of the story and a calling card for what I was up to.

I had always hoped that I might visit the 392nd's old home at Wendling and see what remained. Jim Marsteller and Cliff Peterson gave me a good idea of what to look for and how to proceed. Jim also suggested I visit the Second Division Memorial Library in Norwich. Then, besides the Lorraine Cemetery in France, a third idea for a visit was brewing. Jim had made contact with the acting burgermeister of Ettenheimmunster for Cliff Peterson but Cliff's plans were still uncertain. Jim urged me to go to Germany and visit the scene of the crashes and this idea had a strong appeal to me. My wife and I had secured five-day Eurail passes for the trip and I saw it would be possible to get close to Ettenheim by taking a train directly from St. Avold to Metz and then on to Strasbourg just west of my destination.

I wrote to the German official and told him who I was, enclosing the recent newspaper article. I advised him of my travel plans and said that if someone could act as a translator and show me the crash sites, graveyard and church, I would like to make a visit. Franz Helle phoned me back and with some difficulty with the English, extended a very gracious offer to Mr. and Mrs. McGuire to come visit. I was overjoyed. Bernadette looked a little wary however.

Seeing the German location was important to my research. I also hoped to learn more about the final few mysteries of March 18, 1944. Who was buried where exactly? What was the third plane on the mountaintop and what happened to its crew? Why was one of the bodies, the one not burned, removed by the Luftwaffe and who was it? Finally, why had Wallace's name popped up as among the dead and the living simultaneously?

There was no idle curiosity in these questions. I simply believed that I could never know with any real certainty what happened to any of the dead, including those on #117, unless I determined what happened to all of them.

On Saturday, June 10, 1995, the car that was to take us to JFK airport arrived forty-five minutes late. Then we found out the hard way that the arrangements with British Air were the equivalent of being standbys. Not to worry! We were the last to board, and after two glasses of good champagne in the comfort of oversized lounge chairs, it didn't seem so bad to either of us. From all that we could tell, business class didn't seem much different from first class.

It occurred to me for the first time that if we held to our schedule we would be at the French cemetery a week from Sunday, the 18th. "That's Father's Day," I told my wife.

Closing my eyes, I tried to sort out my feelings. Along with the excitement and expectation, I recognized a strong sense of the inevitable about this trip and all that had led up to it. Although I didn't know exactly what to expect in Europe, I was very calm and confident that it would all work out.

Then we were airborne, on an undefined mission, searching for the final chapters in a story of American generations in a world that still could not keep the peace but was justifiably terrified of war.

Just who was The Navigator? Who was this man that I had grown up wondering about? What did the son, a man himself now, know of his father as he rushed over the Atlantic to stand beside his grave?

All I had were the fleeting glimpses that I was given through the memory of others. It began with my mother, who on occasion would soften in her resolve to shut off the window of the past from my view. Catching my profile, my smile, or even my bushy eyebrows, she would open up to me for a few seconds that I reminded her of my father. Once, in my teen years, as we walked along on a happy evening out, I whistled *Stardust*, and she told me, "That was our wedding song when I married your dad."

With my mother's death and the deaths of other family members, photos, papers and memorabilia connected to my dad came into my possession. Sometimes I studied them with great care and interest. Other times, I put them away quickly, to be rediscovered on other days when I felt more settled and up to dealing with the information. And once in a while I just didn't see what was there in front of me, the details and implications being a kind of commitment that I wasn't able or ready to make.

Though the file was thin and fading like the military records it predated, it grew. And the collective weight of it called out for review and gave me a solid portrait of more than one dimensional quality.

My father was born in Brooklyn on January 9, 1916, to John J. McGuire and Agnes Kinsella McGuire, and baptized at Our Lady of Perpetual Help on the 23rd.

The lanky, long-limbed boy in the First Communion and confirmation photos looked much like the Bill McGuire who would go through the same rituals some twenty-five years later. So did the adolescent, with dark brown hair, in a snapshot behind the wheel of a 1920s roadster in the early Depression years, and the one with the varsity sweater in front of an antique gas pump.

There were a number of team photos from Grandma McGuire's scrapbook. She would on occasion take it out to show it to me when I made one of my rare visits. Not just excelling, but the idea of teamwork was ingrained in my father's nature.

He came from the conservative Catholic tradition of that time that seriously pursued scholarship and viewed it at the same time as a vanity, and a potentially dangerous occupation that might lure a man into easy rationalization and possible conflict with authority and church teaching. He was a moralist, who tried to live by a tough personal code of behavior. He was also a healthy young man who loved a good time and the company of friends.

Among the crumbling scrapbook items was as essay that he had written in high school entitled, "Reverie on the Rosary" for the St. Michael's *Michaelog*. It was a kind of short story about the comfort prayer had brought to an old widowed man throughout his life. William McGuire of the Class of '34 is listed on the masthead as a literary editor.

In September 1994, I was contacted by Floridian and former Eighth Air Force B24 navigator Jack Olsen. Jack had seen the ad in *Retired Officer*'s magazine and phoned. He came up to New York to visit his mother in a nursing home and the two of us had lunch at Sardi's near my office. Jack, a couple of years younger than my father, had grown up in the old Brooklyn neighborhood and in the late 1930s was a regular with Pete McLaughlin in their card game circle at the Our Lady of Perpetual Help church men's club and the McLaughlin kitchen, where young Muriel "Mick" McLaughlin could also be found on occasion. In fact, Jack now told me that he signed up with the Air Corps to become a navigator because Lieutenant McGuire had told him what a great program it was. Hardly anyone had taken that route, since the usual track was to wash out as a pilot first.

Some years before this meeting, at a funeral for another of the McLaughlin brothers, my Uncle Joe, I was approached by another old basketball and card-playing friend of my father's. This man spoke of my dad's legendary smile. He said that my father had been basically a pretty shy guy when it came to the girls. But his smile would light up a room, so his buddies would bring Bill to the bar, buy him a drink, get him laughing and boom, there it was. And soon, so were the girls. Everyone was happy; he never caught on.

Evidently, he had a mind of his own and did not have great patience for windy, high fallutin' arguments. His brother James, nicknamed Buddy, remembered how in the early 1930s he had given a long dissertation to Bill about why Mussolini really wasn't so bad after all. Buddy was really into this and thought he had done a great job. He was eager to take his brother on point by point when he finally did finish. There was a pause. Bill looked at him and said, "You're wrong." Then he got up and left.

Bill Sr. attended Brooklyn College, playing varsity basketball for three years under coaches "Dutch" Connor and Artie Musicant. He captained the team in his senior season, 1937-38. Because of a piece of adhesive tape stuck to his locker with an old name on it, they started calling him "Rip". He hated that but, like the tape, it stuck. Early in his sophomore year he was offered a bona fide three-year ride at George Washington University. But he didn't want to leave family and friends. Couldn't see himself anywhere but Brooklyn. For his all-around leadership in basketball he was presented with the Abe Ratzan memorial award in 1938 and the Boylan-Lubar trophy at Brooklyn College.

Bill majored in English literature, though by the end of his four years he was thinking about a graduate course at New York University in order to become a physical education instructor. One more thing, given a choice of a set shot or a drive to the basket, he'd take the layup every time.

The scrapbook shows him listed among the Brooklyn College graduation class in the local newspaper on June 27, 1938. But he never acknowledged having his bachelor's degree. Gerry McGuire remembered some of the story and brother Buddy agreed. There had been a dispute with one professor for a required course. As a result, this man placed a demand on the student that he, in conscience, didn't feel he could meet. Speaking of the professor, he told his brothers, "He was wrong."

So he became for me a moralist and a bit of a romantic. But they draft that kind too, and in April 1941, Bill was in basic training with the Fourth Armored Division, U.S. Army, Camp Upton and Pine Camp, N.Y. The future navigator was learning radio and how to drive a tank. He sent young sister Rosemary a little pine scented pillow from the P.X. It showed a log cabin with smoke rising from the chimney, by a stream and a canoe. "My Little Home in the Pines, Watertown, N.Y.," the caption read; but not for long.

On February 7, 1942, Bill married Muriel Patricia McLaughlin at Our Lady of Perpetual Help church. His eldest brother Jack officiated. "Mick" in white satin was surrounded by her cousin Doris Leonard, brother Pete's wife, Helen, Bill's sister Rosemary, and their friend Mary Devaney. Mary's husband, Owen Devaney, was the best man and brother Buddy, Mick's brother Bill McLaughlin, and friend Walter "Buck" O'Neill, rounded out the groom's side.

The reception was at the Bay Ridge Hofbrau on 86th Street. Then the couple honeymooned in Bermuda, where Mick skidded on her motor bike in the sand and came home black and blue.

Bill managed to transfer to the Army Air Corps at the end of the summer of '42 while he was with the Armored at Fort Knox, Kentucky. Mick had spent some time with him there after Pearl Harbor. The transfer came with a long furlough home, plus the prospect of becoming an officer, with better pay, and flying. Then there was more training, Air Force style, at the Tyndall Field gunnery school, Panama City, Florida. After six months at the Gulf Coast Training Center, Randolph Field, Texas, and Hondo, Texas, he became an aerial navigator, graduating June 1, 1943. Then it was Clovis, New Mexico; Pueblo, Colorado; Salina and Topeka, Kansas. In the meantime, he had also become an April Fools' Day father.

That summer, Mick came out to Kansas to be with him, leaving me in the care of Grandma McLaughlin. That was the couple's last time together before a brief reunion on his way to embark for England in October.

One of the pieces of paper that I got hold of in the 1980s had a special resonance for me. In practicing public relations I had often created forms for organization employees to use to provide information for potential publicity purposes. The Army had theirs too, of course, and while Lieutenant McGuire was at Wendling in January 1944, he filled one out. Now his son had a copy of those fountain-penned responses.

Lieutenant McGuire listed his CHIEF CIVILIAN OCCUPATION as shipyards and as SECONDARY, salesman. LAST PLACE OF BUSINESS, Bethlehem Steel, Brooklyn. TYPE OF BUSINESS, ship repair. FOREIGN LANGUAGES (Speak, Write, Read), French (a little). FAVORITE SPORTS, basketball, baseball, football. AUTHORS, Chesterton, St. Exupery. MOVIE STARS, Ronald Colman, Spencer Tracy, Jean Arthur, Charles Laughton. FOODS, steak, fried chicken. RECREATION, billiards, bowling, poker.

Finally, there was a listing of hometown newspapers where news of the young airman's exploits might be sent. This was the file, until I received a cache of letters in the year following my trip to Europe.

My wife and I, two tuckered-out travelers, arrived in our London hotel room about 10:30 p.m. and ordered club sandwiches from room service. They came with a fried egg between the slices, which I assumed was some local custom. We slept late Sunday. Then we explored the Knightsbridge area and the edges of nearby Hyde Park. We had lunch in an "authentic" Paris-bistro style restaurant, laughing at the irony that our first true meal in England was French. Then a two-hour bus tour of the city, including "tea" served to the tourists in their seats. We two Americans wanted to slow-motion the sights as the bus rattled through the city and the guide rapid-fired fact after fact.

That night, an unseasonably cold and windy one, we wandered the Covent Garden area looking for a place for supper. We passed a spot that looked like it had possibilities but couldn't find it again later when we tried to turn back on the irregular streets. We sought help from two Bobbies and stepped into a Monty Python comedy. The constables on patrol (COPS) explained that they were really from another station house and worked another neighborhood. Their station was being painted and they were there just to pick up their pay. The steady banter continued for five minutes while they radioed the station house for some help. They argued with the station officer as he consulted the phone directory, accusing him of not knowing how to spell. Eventually we found our way to the well-seasoned coziness of "Rules." The sign on the entrance announced that it was the oldest restaurant in London (ca.1798). It turned out to be a great old room, specializing in game. It played host to a mixture of tourists and decidedly English types.

The next morning, we saw the fabulous food court at Harrod's and shopped for a pair of jeans for Bernadette. We checked out of our hotel, leaving most of our stuff in storage and taxied in one of those great black cabs to Liverpool Street station. I loved the head room. It took me back to the way cars were when I was a boy.

This was our first glimpse from the inside at a European-style open glass and metalwork train station and Bernadette was quite taken with it. While we waited for our departure, I asked for iced tea in a crowded pub where the man behind the counter and several customers looked at me like I had three heads. "Ice?" We both had beers.

Soon we were settled in our train seats, watching June-lush, low-rolling countryside pass by. There were Guernseys and Brahma cows, sheep, wheat, barley, beets, and some corn for feed. Typical Norman-style church towers were part of almost every hamlet, high above the rest of the terrain. One of the last big towns, Ipswich, was right on the waterfront.

We pulled into Norwich about 4 p.m., checked into our hotel and went directly to the Second Air Division Memorial Library. We were introduced to the American-born chief librarian, Phyllis Dubois, and her able assistants, Christine and Leslie. The military library is in a corner of the public library, in temporary quarters in what had been an old furniture store. The original libraries had burned down several years earlier, with many volumes and war memorabilia lost.

We spent two hours signing the visitors' book, seeing the collection, and poring over various documents and accounts of the 392nd Bomb Group. The Second Division Library was established and is supported by an independent foundation. I understood it to be primarily funded and directed through its own board, by Second Division vets and those connected to it.

The library is a great resource for the Eighth family and for researchers. Watching the public come and go while we were there, we could also see that it was a continuing wellspring for local people, especially the young, in renewing ties to long-ago times and to the Americans who had fought for them and with them. Mentioning the Eighth in East Anglia, we learned, was an occasion for profound and immediate respect and honest affection even today. There was a large model of a B24 hanging down on threads over the main desk of the library. I saw a boy about ten walk into the room and approach it, staring in wonderment. The expression on his face as he was transported to another time was memorable.

From a pub a few streets away, we called for a cab to take us across Norwich to the Georgian House on Unthank Road. We passed the ruins of the Roman wall which once surrounded the town and saw in the distance the tower of Norwich Cathedral, the second tallest spire in England. The hotel itself, once a boys boarding school, was directly across the street from the Catholic Cathedral Church of St. John the Baptist, a late 19th century addition to the medieval town. By comparison, Norwich Cathedral dates from the 12th century. We had dinner in the hotel and called it an early night.

The next morning was gray and cold, with a stiff breeze and intermittent drizzle. The library had contacted a volunteer to drive us the twenty odd miles to Wendling. While waiting, we crossed the road to the massive walls of St. John's. The church followed the 13th century English Gothic style and featured a chapel devoted to St. Joseph. It served as the seat of the Roman Catholic Diocese of East Anglia including the counties of Norfolk, Suffolk, and Cambridgeshire. One of the side altars was dedicated to Our Lady of Perpetual Help, and there was the same framed print of the Madonna and Child that I remembered from the first grade. I lit a candle here, the first of many we would light together in England, France and Germany. And as I did, I could only wonder if my father had stood there praying as well, fifty years before.

Promptly at 10 a.m., our driver and escort arrived to take us to the old air base. Derek Patfield, though in his mid-seventies, seemed a much younger man in every respect. He was bright, dignified, down to earth, sweet, funny, and elfin. A retired engineer, he made and flew kites for a hobby, part of a group of local enthusiasts. We also learned that Derek was a bombardier on a Lancaster during the war and flew thirty-three missions. He was the only member of his original crew to survive the war unscathed. We three became friends in the course of the day.

At the tranquil and beautiful small memorial area at Wendling, with its stone obelisk dedicated to the dead of the 392nd, we were met by our guide, Denis Duffield. He explained that the 392nd got the jump on many of the other bomb groups in establishing an appropriate monument for a simple reason. They passed the hat around the base before the fellows went home in June of '45.

Denis had grown up on the edge of the base and was in his early teens at the end of the war. He was adopted as an unofficial mascot by the men of the 392nd and given a leather jacket with insignia when they left. A retired green grocer and delivery van driver, he has been escorting people around the old property for almost a half century.

The memorial plot and monument has, in recent years at the urging of the vets, come under the supervision of the American Battle Monuments Commission. The land was originally loaned out by local property owners and more recently became a permanent gift to the foundation that supports the monument. With the Stars and Stripes and the Union Jack audibly snapping from masts that flanked the obelisk, Denis explained that almost 800 men had lost their lives over the short history of this base.

In theory, the base would have four squadrons of twelve B24's each. Each day part of the force would stand down or not fly for various reasons while the others would be operational. In practice, due to losses, mechanical failure, damage repair, and delays in delivery of new ships on order, the normal flying strength in the winter of 1943-44 would have been closer to twenty-four ships. In addition to the fliers, there were maintenance, technical, support, and administrative personnel giving the base the total population of a small town or college campus, about 3,000.

Very little was left for us to see, but we were more interested in the atmosphere, the sense of the place and of the land than in artifacts alone. For me, there was still a restless energy dormant there in these rural fields. The more I saw, the more I felt that.

We drove to various places on the perimeter of the old air field, then went by foot from there. Behind some houses we saw moss covered Quonset huts, which the British called Nissen huts. They were still being used by property owners as storage sheds but did not seem to have much life left in them. At ground level, still intact, was a reinforced concrete bomb shelter meant to hold several hundred people in much the same way a Manhattan subway car might accommodate the same number on any given morning at 8:35 a.m. Wendling and the surrounding area had been hit by the Germans several times, twice badly with loss of life, Denis said.

Derek opted to sit out, while Denis drove us toward the only concrete strip that remains. The biggest commercial enterprise on the property today is a large turkey farm. We made our way around the huge sheds that housed the birds.

The diagrams of the old base that I have seen make it look something like a Christmas ham all wrapped up for delivery. Three strings, the runways, crisscross its surface. The oblong shape stretches roughly east to west. One string runs from bottom to top, true north, dissecting the package. Running across the length of the package, from the narrow shank in the southeast through to its widest point in the northwest, is the main runway.

As we drove around the end of the turkey sheds, we came onto the runway. We began to pick up speed over the course of the mile-long run. Our car was surrounded by new-green spring crops. Denis explained that one of the reasons this strip remained, while the other two had been cannibalized over the years, was that it continued to serve a purpose. It divided the property of two farmers who did not hold one another in very high regard.

On the edge of the runway red poppies grew, tall and graceful, startling against the slate sky. Denis pointed out a rise in the distance, a mound, now greatly reduced by those using it for landfill. This was originally intended for gunnery practice, test bursts before takeoff, he said.

Most of the base installation buildings are gone also. Some small businesses occupy those remaining or the parts of those remaining. With the permission of the owner of a used Jaguar parts dealer, the four of us went around back to a small garage. Some years earlier the owner had stripped one old wall of paneling and found a mural underneath depicting B24s and a large eagle insignia. This had been the 392nd Combat Officers Club and mess. Bernadette snapped a flash photo.

We moved onto the old command complex and saw the facility was still in use, although Bernadette and I got the distinct impression that its office workers were ready for more up-to-date accommodations. On the property of a John Deere farm equipment dealer, Denis showed us the brick foundation of the old control/observation tower. And the clear spot where a single brick had been removed by him and others.

The brick, with others from the U.S. bases in England, became part of a precisely reconstructed tower at the Air Force museum at Wright-Patterson air base near Dayton, Ohio. Speaking of the wartime, Denis remembered scanning the skies for the return of the 392nd. Particularly in the warmer months, when the light lasted, the people in the countryside, just like the Army Air Force big shots up in the tower, would watch and wait to count the Liberators that made it back from their raids on the continent.

It was my pleasure to buy the boys lunch at the Ploughshare in Beeston, a short distance away, and one of the 392nd's favorite watering holes during the war. We shared warm local English beer in the authentic low-slung pub room. A new dining addition had been added to the back of the original tavern. But we stayed up front and had pea soup and "on-the-bone" ham sandwiches. Denis took me to an alcove behind and to the left of the bar. It was a space dedicated to the men of the 392nd, with photos, poems, and letters of those who had served there and had not forgotten.

We sat there and talked for a good hour or more about how it had been back then. Periodically, there was laughter. And too, we got a wee bit weepy-eyed. Denis and Derek also enjoyed the presence of Bernadette McGuire. For me it was just a great time. My wife took a picture of us just outside this place that could have taken its name from the biblical injunction, "And they shall beat their swords into ploughshares."

The rain and wind had picked up as we said goodbye to Denis. The bombardier, who had tee-totaled during lunch, drove us back to Norwich, showing us some of the town and the old servicemen's dance hall. He spoke of the sensitivity of those days to the socializing of the English girls with the loud and free-spending G.I.s. "Our American friends," the young women called them, he said. I remembered the old British barb about the Americans: "Overpaid, oversexed, and over here."

The alliance, we gathered, was never easy, particularly in overcrowded, tightly rationed, badly bruised England prior to the invasion. But in the end they all realized it was the only way to beat the Hun.

Bernadette and I decided to change hotels and leave the next morning. But the place we chose was overbooked. So we caught the next train to London and had supper in the dining car, talking endlessly about what we had seen.

We found a good hotel room in London's Marylebone district, the second place we tried. I transported our remaining luggage from Knightsbridge. We slept soundly and late.

Late morning, Wednesday, the 14th , found us at St. Paul's Cathedral. To us it was a beautiful and impressive place, but as much a shrine to the old notions of empire as it was to Christian devotion. For it was full of statues and the remains of those who had extended the boundaries of the British idea.

We found our primary objective there, behind the main altar. It was a small chapel dedicated to all the American service people in WWII who had come out of England to die in the European Theater. Facing the chapel altar, and directly to the rear of the main altar, is a glass-encased, heavy, gilded red leather volume laying open. Therein, in beautiful calligraphy, are the names and ranks of these same dead, in alphabetical order. There were columns of names but not the right one for me. I wanted to lift the glass lid and turn the pages, but it was locked.

A constant flow of tourists passed through the stately old church. Bernadette and I went up the wooden steps to the famous Whispering Gallery in the first ring of the rotunda. The elevator was, of course, out. Though it was still cool, it was humid and the two of us were a little winded on reaching the top. Bernadette rested on a rotunda bench and was amused by a large contingent of tourists, East Asian nuns or novices, who acted much like giggling schoolgirls. I pushed onward and upward over the 600 plus steps to the very top of the cathedral.. At various points the steps led out onto the exterior upper reaches of the dome that Christopher Wren had built. I looked out on the town and the Thames and marveled at what we had learned on our earlier bus tour, how a special team of volunteers had labored around the clock to protect the church during the blitz, quickly putting out nearby fires and shoring up wherever necessary.

Lunch was at Wheeler's, a seafood restaurant near the Tower of London. We met a couple from Atlanta at the next table. Then it was the Tower tour, highlighted by our mustachioed, informative, entertaining and very human guide, a Tower Beefeater, in full regalia.

For the first time, the weather was pleasant. Or, almost pleasant, depending on how long the sunshine avoided the clouds and the wind paused. We were fascinated by the history of the fortress and the various buildings that are its components. To the two of us, it was certainly more impressive by far than the glass enclosed and theatrically presented crown jewels. This riveting history was greatly epitomized by the chapel, St. Peter-in-Chains, which Queen Victoria ordered restored and reconsecrated around mid-19th century.

Within the confines of the fortress, something like thirty-three nobles had been executed according to the record. Just outside the walls, in contrast, on Execution Hill, many many other poor souls were unceremoniously dispatched. But following the Queen's order, the renovators searched under the floor of St. Peter's and found the unrecorded remains of more than a thousand others who had found themselves on the wrong side of the crown or its officers. The Beefeater said that they had all been reburied there, with solemn honors. "Things were not always so merry in merry old England," I whispered to my wife.

The two of us noticed something about authentic London pubs. They remain, despite tourists and '90s urbanity, largely clubby places for regulars. More than once, as we entered the smallish pub, the raucous noise level would immediately fall away, glasses would in a motion be lowered or set on the bar, cigarette smokers would pause, and all heads as one would turn to the newly arrived. Count one-two-three beats, and then the faces would turn away, the noise resume, and the glasses and smokes would be realigned in their natural places, close to the lip. To us, it was as if Londoners had been thoroughly briefed on this procedure.

So, weary and wandering after a day of touring, we had a hard time deciding where to have a pick-me-up. Near Piccadilly, I finally pulled the two of us to the beacon of the Ritz Hotel. We were hardly across the thickly carpeted lobby floor when we were intercepted by an oily, officious representative of the establishment who informed me, with cheerful superiority, that we could not drink in any of the three bars on the ground floor or otherwise stay in the hotel because I was wearing jeans! I thought of the wonderful irony of it. I didn't have long flowing hair and beard, facial tattoos, or rings through my lips and tongue, but such people could drink at the Ritz and I couldn't. Outside, I said to my wife in final protest, "But I never wear jeans!" I had, however, that day.

We found a lovely Italian restaurant nearby that was much more simpatico. Wine and *pasta carbonara*, cooked perfectly *al dente* in chafing dishes right next to the table, soothed my disposition and topped off a wonderful London day.

Later we would learn that a drink at the Ritz may have once saved my father's life, fifty years before.

On June 15, we left Waterloo Station on the Eurostar train bound for the Channel Chunnel and Paris. It was too crowded and disorganized, with no proper place for luggage. But otherwise the trip was fast, smooth, and impressive. Two hours and forty-five minutes later we were driving from Gare du Nord in a cab toward our Paris hotel on the left bank, near the Louvre, in the St. Germain de Pres section.

The next day, Friday, we took a tour of the city which included bus sight-seeing, three neighborhood walks, a long boat ride on the Seine with lunch, music and dancing, and an exclusive visit to a fine museum in a mansion, the Jacquemart-Andre.

The comfortable bus level view of the City of Light was ideal for a couple of weary travelers and the day was warm, sunny, and perfectly beautiful. The evening stayed balmy, and we walked up the broad Boulevard St. Germain past the crowded cafés and had supper in a busy family-style restaurant just across from the oldest church in the city, began on that spot in 542. St. Germain-des-Pres was part of a large and famous Benedictine abbey which was suppressed during the Revolution, with most of its buildings destroyed by fire in 1794. Two years earlier, a mob had attacked the nearby monastery slaughtering 318 priests who lived there.

Paris was magnificent in every aspect. Its 19th century reconstruction created a kind of bourgeois ideal of broad tree-lined avenues, beautiful parks and buildings that conformed to a certain height and uniformity of style. Rather than being monotonous, this complemented the older structures and neighborhoods and was most graceful and human. It all quite simply swept us off our feet. After dinner we sipped champagne on the sidewalk of the Café de Flore and watched the world pass by.

Saturday, we explored, walking across an ornate river bridge to the Louvre side, and over to the old Les Halles, or market district. After a late breakfast in a cheery brasserie, we walked in, through and around St. Eustache's Church, a building of Gothic design with Renaissance detail. It was built over a hundred-year period beginning in 1532. There was a wedding in progress while we were there. This church struck the both of us as a powerfully holy place.

We strolled on through the narrow streets, past the open markets and the not very attractive Pompidou Center, then worked our way to the Cathedral of Notre Dame. It had seemed closer than it really was. When we finally got to the entrance doors they were locked. There was a sign: Closed for lunch. The two of us thought that hilarious!

After a coffee, we entered the church which was crowded with tourists and worshipers. Notre Dame was dark and musty in its antiquity. The gorgeous stained glass rose windows were startlingly rich in contrast. Afterward, we walked back along the right bank past the flower market and the zoological market, a symbol of sorts of the lasting cornucopia the city represents. The river too, with its wide banks flanked by well-pruned trees and magnificent bridges, seemed almost timelessly serene in its meandering purpose.

That evening we met old friends, Joe and Mary Bohan, just arrived in the city from our hometown. We all had dinner in the wonderful Le Procope, which began, it is said, as the original café and evolved into a slightly touristy but very nice restaurant. Napoleon and Ben Franklin used to pop in now and then for some java. Le Procope dates to 1686, and is the oldest continuous dining establishment in the city. We found it just terrific to see familiar faces and converse in good old American after a week in Europe.

We missed one train Sunday morning from Gare de L'Est for St. Avold, Lorraine. With an hour or more to kill, the two of us surveyed a nearby park and discovered a lovely canal, with a delicate high arched bridge and the bateaux that regularly cruised there.

Though we had checked before boarding with the information booth, the ticket clerk, and the conductor, we found out that our expensive Eurail pass did not guarantee seats for the four hour-plus train ride. The train had been sold out and no one we asked had informed us we would need reservations. A second conductor told us, "You cannot ride on this train" and, "This is not my problem." But we stubbornly found a place to plunk our luggage at the rear end of the dining car. We waited until it was open for business and were greeted warmly, until they saw the luggage. A definite no-no. So we went back to our spot and later took turns dining solo to rest the legs while the other guarded our property. The train chugged eastward through interesting countryside.

The schedule was off some as well, so we arrived at the little St. Avold train station late in the afternoon. There were no cabs. All the cars there to pick up people quickly disappeared. Then we were virtually alone. No one spoke English. I did not relish struggling with the coinage and the information operator when I don't do that particularly well in my own country. But the ticket agent figured out what was going on and called a cab for us. Many mercis later we arrived at our hotel, checked in, plunked down our luggage, and called for another cab to the cemetery.

It had been drizzling and raining off and on with wild clouds racing across the horizon. But as we entered the gates of the Lorraine American Cemetery and Memorial, the rain stopped, the wind died and the sun pierced through the clouds. We were greeted at the main reception center by Mr. Gebhart, the French custodian, who spoke in perfect English. He checked his computer to verify that we had the right grave location. He prepared an information folder for us and then drove us to a path near the gravesite. It was near the tall rectangular memorial chapel and tower, and the U.S. flag, among rows and rows of white marble crosses and Stars of David.

Gebhart went around to the back of the station wagon and removed two pails, also slinging a camera over his shoulder.

Without explanation, he carried the pails, one of which seemed to have a towel on top, the other water, up toward the graves. We followed, containing our mutual puzzlement. Then we stood before the cross that said: *William C. J. McGuire, 2 LT, 579 Bomb Sq., 392 Bomb Group, New York, Mar 18 1944. Plot A. Row 23. Grave 40.*

Gebhart placed the buckets and the camera down near the cross, explaining that so many people have problems with their own cameras and end up disappointed that the Monuments Commission decided to provide visitors with a Polaroid memento of the site. As he spoke he washed dirt and grass from the marble. Then he took handfuls of sand from the second bucket and moistening these, pressed them into the engraving to bring out the letters for the camera. He took the picture and said he would have it in the frame for us when we returned to the reception area.

Then we were alone at the grave. After a while we walked among the other stones and up to the chapel. We passed two sets of brothers to the right of my father's grave, forming a square. We learned there were twenty-eight brothers there, all buried side by side. Most of the dead here, on these 116 acres constructed by the Seventh Army, are infantry from the final push of the late fall and winter of 1944. Among them are 151 unknown soldiers. Walking up the slope to the tower we passed low flanking walls on which were inscribed the name, rank, organization, and home state of 444 missing of the Army and Air Corps. The Wall of the Missing commemorates those whose remains were not recovered or identified.

Above the entrance of the tower or chapel is the twenty-six foot high sculpture of St. Avold, also called St. Nabor. Avold was a Roman soldier of Emperor Maximian who refused to deny his Christian faith and was martyred for that conviction. He extends his hands in blessing on all the dead memorialized here. On his side is a sheathed sword. Above his head floats an Archangel with trumpet in hand.

We easily pushed open the huge bronze doors and entered into the chapel. We were alone. On the west wall directly opposite the doors was a kind of altar with a mural above of a sculpted group of historical figures: David, Constantine, Arthur, Washington. They are meant to represent the age old struggle for freedom. The group is dominated by a youthful figure in the center who looks down on them as his right arm reaches up into the unknown. Beneath is the inscription: "Our fellow countrymen—enduring all and giving all that mankind might live in freedom and in peace. They join the glorious band of heroes who have gone before."

On the left or south wall was a colorful glazed ceramic war map showing the invasion force and subsequent battles for the European continent. Above the huge map and on the opposite north wall were the military units' battle flags. At the rear wall was an inscription from Eisenhower's dedication of the same "Golden Book" we had seen at St. Paul's Cathedral:

Here we and all who shall hereafter live in freedom will be reminded that to these men and their comrades we owe a debt to be paid, with grateful remembrance of their sacrifice and with the high resolve that the cause for which they died shall live.

To the right of the doors was the simple dedicatory inscription that gripped me in a wave of sudden emotion as I read:

In proud remembrance of the achievements of her sons and in humble tribute to their sacrifices this memorial has been erected by the United States of America.

Lorraine is the largest American WWII cemetery in Europe. A total of 10,481 American service men and eight service women are buried here. Bernadette and I made our way back to the Navigator's resting place.

I spoke aloud to my father's grave, holding my wife's hand. Light rain began to fall once again and it was past the closing time for the cemetery. I told my father that I had had a good life and a wonderful family and that I hoped some day we would be together once more. We said a brief prayer. I kissed the top of the cross, and with my arm around Bernadette, we left.

We passed the grave of a man killed on Christmas Day 1944. I thought of the inscription in the green marble base of the chapel altar memorial. It was *John 10: 28*, "I give unto them eternal life and they shall never perish."

The next morning we took the train to Metz. We took a long walk there, enjoying the pretty neatness of the old city, while we waited for the connecting train to Strasbourg. At the platform there we were met by Franz Josef Helle and his wife, Ula, short for Ursula, who presented Bernadette with a single long-stemmed yellow rose. It was to be the most beautiful day of the trip, with sunny blue skies and temperatures pushing into the mid 80s.

We had an almost instant rapport with the Helles, who were five to ten years younger than we are. Franz was sandy-haired, stocky, with a full, closely-trimmed beard. He was not the mayor of Ettenheimmunster, he explained; the village along with several others was incorporated into the larger political unit of Ettenheim, and there sat the overall mayor, Bruno Metz. Franz was the local official, or magistrate, whose title in English translated into something like "the man who stands before the town." He seemed a very capable and gregarious fellow. Ula was slim, attractive and vivacious. She had been born and raised in Canada and the States but the family came back to Germany before she started school. The ability of the two couples to communicate, since both the hosts had some English, was good and it grew from hour to hour in the time we were together.

The Helles drove us in their car, across the plain of the Rhine and over the river into Germany. The Rhine struck me as not very wide there and rather placid in comparison to our Hudson. There was no border check for passport or I.D. at either end of our trip.

They picked up the autobahn for about twenty minutes, apologizing to us for some traffic, as we made our way east to an exit near Ettenheim. Then on a few miles more to Ettenheimmunster. Franz said the village had about 1,200 residents with about 6,000 in the immediate area beyond. The village is in a small valley with a little stream running through it. On either side, small mountains, about the size of the Catskills, rise up with a covering of evergreens and other trees. These hills and mountains are the edge of the Black Forest. The mountain on the northern flank is where "Sinister Minister," "Big Time Operator," and an unknown B17 came down, March 18, 1944.

The Helles settled us into the village Gasthaus, the Sonne, or Sun, and after storing our gear and freshening up, we met again in the dining room for a cold drink. Franz introduced us there to Marga Kohr, a journalist for the local paper. Then we all set off up the mountain in two cars along a winding rutted dirt road. Climbing rapidly, we looked back down through the trees at sudden dizzying drops and sumptuous vistas.

According to Franz Helle's homework, which was based on the Army's report and map, and the memory of locals, #117 was the lowest in elevation of the three crash sites. Franz stopped the car and we all got out. He pointed up into the woods to a spot about 100 yards off the road and then he and I climbed up the steep incline while the three women stood on the road and watched.

There wasn't much undergrowth because of the pines. I stood there talking with Franz, the both of us with hands on hips like we were supervising something. The forest had had a half century to recover. There was not a trace of the violence that had once visited this grove. Franz went back to the women, and turning my back to them, I walked a little further on into the woods. There was only the sounds of songbirds, the steady hum of hundreds of bees, and the ancient stillness of the trees. I suppose I could have looked harder or a little more carefully. In retrospect, I might have brought along a metal detector or at least a shovel to look for artifacts. But in truth, these things never entered my mind, for although I had prepared myself for the possibility of troubling information on this trip, what I was actually experiencing was a growing and almost overwhelming sense of peace.

Franz spoke of the damage of acid rain to the forest as we drove up and around to our second destination. On a kind of small plateau, further up the slope above the first crash site, was the place Peterson's "Big Time Operator" came down. The top of the mountain here was called Koecherhof by the locals for the family and enclave that had once, very long ago, been established on this spot. Now, it was almost all trees except for a small field, a clearing that had in recent times been used by some squatters or "hippies," the Helles explained. This is about 300 yards across the plateau from where the Peterson plane landed and near where the Koecherhof home had once been.

Franz pointed out the place where the wartime hut had been. This was where the teacher, Valentin Strickfaden, had met up with the three American airmen. A hunting blind was also there, elevated on stilts above the ground, on the edge of the clearing. We saw several in the area. Franz told us that hunters still take small-to-large game here, including deer and wild boar. The body of Enoch Masters had also been found nearby.

I had asked about what was known of Masters and the one unburned body that had been removed from the crash site for burial at Lahr, but Franz said he could learn nothing more than what was in the record. Some villagers who were still around had memories of these things, but all the principals who had been deposed after the war were now dead, he said, including Pastor Merkle, Mayor Tisch, and Valentin Strickfadden.

Across the top of the ridge, perhaps a mile away, we came to the third site, where the B17 had come in. It was in another clearing on the edge of a rocky outcropping. If the Fortress had fallen a bit lower, it would have tumbled down the sheer side of the mountain. Nearby was a dark sand stone marker, engraved to commemorate an agreement for the use of the mountain by the surrounding towns. It dated from the first decade of the 19th century. I took a photo there of the others in our party. We then made our way back down to the Ettenheimmunster cemetery, just above the village at the foot of the mountain. Journalist Marga Kohr bid farewell. Taking my hand, she said to both Bernadette and me, "You are strong people. I admire that."

The small, "new" Ettenheimmunster communal cemetery was about 100 years old, a meticulously kept, intimately beautiful place. Franz said there were about twenty-five family names that were common in the valley through its long recorded history. Most of these were represented here. It was remarkable to me that in wartime they could agree to place the U.S. dead alongside their own in such a familiar setting.

The cemetery was up the slope from the edge of the town about a quarter mile from the village church, St. Landelin, which could be plainly seen through the tall cypress trees. Each of the graves had marble edging around the plot. White stones were set in between and were free of weeds. There was only evidence of love and care here. Many of the plots had planted floral decoration, mostly begonias. Most had small covered votive lights, almost like Japanese lanterns, and similar holders for incense.

Franz took us to one row. He pointed to a headstone for a man named Singler. A glass enclosed service portrait of a uniformed WWII soldier is embedded in it. Franz made a sweeping gesture from this point to the hedge at the end of the property. "Here is where the airmen were buried," he said. "Your father was three from the end by the hedge." I knew that he had learned this from the documents I had sent to him before the trip.

Franz had presented me with a large brown envelope. He held his hand over mine for a moment, explaining. While Helle had been reconnoitering the cemetery with map and notes in hand, in preparation for our visit, an old woman had approached him. "What are you doing?" she asked him directly.

He explained.

She nodded and went away.

Two days later Franz Helle received a phone call. It was the same woman. "You know," she said, "my sister has photographs of that funeral if you would be interested in seeing them."

I reached in the envelope and drew out two fuzzy black and white photographs. One was of a row of eight visible wooden caskets in a trench. At the top, the arms and shovel of the gravedigger ready to do his work. At the bottom, a bowl of holy water and the ornate dispenser with which to sprinkle it. The second print showed the undertaker pulling a casket down boards into the trench. Behind him, the funeral celebrants and witnesses, Father Merkle with white hair and his notched Roman collar. A second priest on the right. The pastor holds open his prayer book. He is flanked by acolytes, altar boys in cassock and white surplice. Processional crucifixes. It was all there. Bell, book, and candle. The brown muddy ground and bare trees of March.

My wife and I were both astounded. It was one thing to be told the story and quite another to be presented with a window on history and to open it and see once again. I began, finally, to hand the photos back. "No," said Franz. "Those are for you. To keep."

Franz and Ula invited us up the mountain a little way to their home. Before going into public service Franz had been in brick laying and construction with his father. He built his own chalet-style home with a large deck overlooking their valley. Bernadette and I got to meet their three sons, and the oldest, Boris, about sixteen, then joined us in our conversations. He was studying English at school, and once and a while he displayed a knowledge of the language that surpassed his father's, much to the amusing chagrin of Franz.

We shared another cold drink and spoke of many things, including family histories, careers, and local lore and legend. Encouraged by me to go on, Franz and Boris told us the story of St. Landelin, to whom the village church was dedicated. Landelin was a red headed, red-bearded Irish monk, "a Celt like you, Bill," Franz said with a smile. Some versions of the tale make him out to be little more than a tramp or a forest hermit. But in the preferred telling, he came to the valley as a solo Christian missionary about 630 A.D. with the avowed purpose of converting the resident pagans.

He did so well at this that one day a local baron grew furious with him and cut off his head with his sword in an angry fit. The story says a spring immediately bubbled up on the spot and continues to this day. Some kind of church has supposedly been there ever since. Just outside the present church, an 18th century masterpiece, a fountain still draws from the same wellspring, the story goes.

Benedictine monks came about a generation later and established a great monastery there. "The ruins of the wall and the entrance gate are up the road by the gasthaus you're staying in," Franz said. He showed me a beautiful color print of what the monastery had looked like in its heyday as a learning center.

At the end of the 18th century, the French, representing the authority that remained of the Holy Roman Empire, cut a deal with the local German barons. In return for certain cities on the French side of the Rhine, the barons could take certain Church properties and monasteries on the German side. A thousand year tradition was eradicated with the stroke of a royal pen.

The priests were sent packing. Eventually the great buildings fell into disrepair and neglect, without a legitimate reason for being. They crumbled and were leveled in the mid 19th century and the land, which had always been farmed, was then used entirely for agriculture. "It still is," Franz explained.

Today, the area is somewhat economically depressed, he continued. The biggest enterprise in the region had been the Royal Canadian Air Base at Lahr. But they shut it down after German reunification. The two biggest "businesses" in the village now are a retirement home for the elderly run by the Church and an alcoholic treatment center for men managed by Caritas, an international relief organization. The patients from the treatment center farm the old monastery land and operate a hot house/nursery near the road by our hotel. So, they continue to live on the land, providing for themselves much as the monks did for a millennium.

"We know a lot about the Benedictine monastery," said Franz. "But Landelin is just a story, a legend. There is no evidence." Both the Helles laughed, a trifle self- consciously. Whatever my reasons, I could not dismiss the story so lightly.

That night Franz and Ula hosted an old fashioned, multi-course, knock down drag out German dinner for us at the Sonne.

The conversation covered a lot of ground, from Frank Capra films to Bosnia. But it kept coming back to the importance of family and the futility of war. There was a seemingly endless supply of fine food and liquid refreshment of marvelous variety. Bernadette and I, when asked about our trip, mentioned our two dinners at the oldest restaurants in Paris and London. The Helles nodded at the dates involved—1798 and 1686— and seemed more amused than truly impressed.

The next day we explored the Church of St. Landelin and saw the story of his martyrdom told in large, successive, ornately-framed murals, or frescos, inset in the ceiling. The distinct gap between the saint's head and his body seemed melodramatic. But there was something touching in the portrayal of the surrounding forest animals as they took in Landelin's beheading. Nature's frozen witnesses to the folly of mankind.

Franz and Ula walked us across the main road through town to Helle's office in the town hall. He showed us a room off the present records room, where the American crash survivors were initially held overnight under lock and key until the Luftwaffe took them away. Opposite the town hall, and forming a U with it, was a building used as a school and another that was the former residence of Father Merkle.

Going up the stairs in the town hall to see the meeting room, I noticed a large picture frame along the staircase wall. It contained a cameo collection with artwork around each photo suggesting the fruit of a tree. Here all the WWII service dead of Ettenheimmunster were honored, with names, service branch, rank, and their uniformed portrait. Just as I had been earlier when I encountered the soldier's gravestone photo inset, I was taken aback by the difference between my reaction to the Nazi-era uniforms and the honor still afforded here to those who wore them.

Franz took us up to some high ground above Ettenheim, a point lookout maintained by a hiking group. From the tower we could see for miles and we realized for the first time just how close these towns and the Rhine really were to each other. We also visited the Cathedral of St. Bartholomew there, and saw the fine graveyard chapel and belfry that Franz and his father had worked on together.

Franz had commitments for the rest of the day but Ula took us to nearby Freiburg, which had experienced considerable bomb damage during the war. It was a beautiful and modern city with a center that, thanks to reconstruction, seems to have stepped out of the late Middle Ages. Some time after 2 p.m., we made our way to a restaurant in an imposingly quaint hotel that Ula had been determined to take us to. Unfortunately, the kitchen was closed until supper time. We looked around the charming, low-slung dining room with its bright table linens contrasting with polished wood settees and hand carved built-ins. Then we followed Ula's sweeping gesture to a plaque on the wall. With the admirable understatement of a dry smile, she pointed to the date. It seemed to say: "Serving since 1306." So much for old restaurants in Paris and London. Bernadette was heard to say with a laugh, "You win." That was the Hotel Baren.

Later I took a photograph of St. Mark's, one of the ancient gates of the city. Bernadette pointed out to me the McDonald's restaurant built into the wall a little further up. Oh, the ugly Americans, I thought. I had been so busy focusing on the past I hadn't even seen it.

We explored the graceful Freiburg Cathedral. Its towers were characterized by a lattice of open masonry fretwork unlike anything we had seen before. Despite some deterioration in the stone of the church, this gave it a light, almost ethereal quality of enhanced spirituality.

We took a break for tea, coffee, and ice cream in an open café in the square in the shadow of the cathedral. Bernadette and I were about to encounter the only decidedly unpleasant German we came across on our visit. The weather was fine once again. We were talking of Ula's side of the family when she dropped her little plastic cigarette lighter. An older, heavy-set German at the next table snatched it up, ignoring Ula's outstretched hand. I had noticed him earlier, with a Rubenesque lady companion, because he kept turning toward our American English with a kind of sneer. He examined Ula's green lighter like it was a bug, rolling it around in his fingers. Ula explained that he had her lighter. He said it was his. She said, "Yours is on the table in front of you." He looked down at this and brushed it with the fingers of his other hand. Then he said something to his tablemate and she brought up her purse and started rummaging through it. Ula meanwhile was rattling on in a calm but metallically insistent German. The woman then pulled out a third green lighter and said something like, "No, here it is!"

The man held up the lighter from the table and squinting, checked the fluid lines on both pieces. Then with a sour expression, but without even looking at Ula, he extended her lighter back. She coolly lit her cigarette, and putting the lighter back in her purse, resumed our conversation. He never offered the slightest word of apology.

The next morning, the bubbling brook that ran past our high bedroom window and the rooster up the slope got us up before the full light of dawn. After a good breakfast, we walked into the village. We went past the original gate to the monastery, the greenhouse and the fields, where reformed drinkers practiced a timeless therapy. We looked beyond the farmland to the dark green mountain where #117 met its final fate. At the Church of St. Landelin, we said a parting prayer.

Franz and Ula took us to lunch at still another local pub. We met the handsomely young and bright Mayor Bruno Metz, who was there only by coincidence. Then we drove on to France and Strasbourg. Checking into a hotel, we bought the Helles a round of drinks and the four of us set out together on foot to explore the many canaled wonders of this remarkable city, where the buildings and narrow streets covered 500 years of architectural styles. There was yet another enormous old cathedral, this one with an ingeniously complex-looking clock that was the 19th century equivalent of CNN and a one-man band. "It told you everything you wanted to know," I said to no one in particular. "As long as you had the instructions on how to read it."

Late that afternoon, we were caught in a thunderstorm and took refuge in a café alongside a canal. Several beers later Franz said, only half joking, "Their beer is not as good as our beer, is this not so?" I laughed, shaking my head at this reminder of ageless rivalry. But Franz, looking somewhat perplexed, still awaited my answer; so I solemnly added, "Yes, this is so."

Outside we all embraced and made our good-byes. That night the two of us had an Alsatian dinner in the oldest quarter of the city, which was once dominated by the centuries-old trade unions or guilds. Then we took a romantic stroll along the water on yet another balmy night. It was the time of the annual pop music festival and there were youngsters, thousands of them in the streets from all over Europe. Everywhere we went we saw crowds, bands, bonfires, and street fairs. The music, indoors and out, was great, from folk to hard rock to progressive jazz. Wherever we walked, when one band would finish another would immediately take its place.

But we were too, too tired to do it all justice, and only after many twists and turns, finally found our way back to the hotel. We were glad the bellhop had talked us into an air-conditioned room and that he had left it on for us.

We could have easily spent another three days in Strasbourg but the next morning we took the train to Paris, back to our old hotel by the Seine.

The following day, Friday, we attacked the city again on foot. Two and a half hours in the Louvre: Winged Victory, Mona Lisa, and Venus de Milo. On our way to the Eiffel Tower we literally ran into a company of French National Guard, all on black horses, in full cavalry regalia. Even the usually blase Parisians came out of shops and onto apartment terraces to see them clip clop down the streets of the Invalides district.

From as high up on the tower as we were allowed, we were astounded at the scope, depth, and reach of this city that we had come to admire so much. I pointed out the shiny dome of Sacre Coeur in Montmartre, the highest point of land in the city and said to my wife, "I'm taking you to lunch there."

We had a simple repast in bright sunshine at the top of the hill in a square behind the church. When I returned from the restroom I found an itinerant portrait painter importuning my wife: "Ah, I have found the new Mona Lisa." Sacre Coeur was a study in contrasts. The area surrounding the outside of the church, and the bottom of the hill, with its Pigalle night clubs and sex shops, was cheap and profane. Yet, to the two of us, the inside of the shrine was a sacred place, of genuine devotion. Its tradition of continuous around-the-clock services had been going on, in war and peace, for more than a hundred years. Together, we lit the last candle in the last church that we would visit in Europe. On Saturday we flew to London and on home to JFK airport.

Looking back on it, Europe more than met my hopes and expectations. I had gathered little new hard information but my sense of the places my father had touched, and to some degree, their people, had been immeasurably sharpened and grounded in detail.

Rather than seeing England, France, and Germany, as tired, decrepit places, to me the Old World was a lesson, a pain-filled lesson in durability and persistence. My wife and I had walked down timeless, well-worn pathways and sought out places that, when discovered, seemed somehow familiar. Churches, shrines, memorials... scenes of devotion, and of conflict and conflagration. Places where the past was palpable, not only around us but within us, inherent in our knowledge of ourselves. Places ripe with the odor of the ground that all the weight of the world rests on. And from high above, we could hear the gargoyles slyly whisper, confirmation that we had been this way before and that the purpose and the meaning remained the same, just as they always were. Jerusalem, Canterbury, Campostela, Mecca, Shangri La, Lourdes. All the same journey, to the same destination. For at the heart of the mystery of the ages of Western Man, that long parade of fools, saints, and sinners, the seeker always finds blood and conscience. Here is the refining crucible, the civilization's holy grail.

Human history, Europe brought home to me, always turns on individual choices, the acts of great men and small, forging common links in an endless chain. A kind of progress works its way sometimes blindly toward freedom and enlightenment, but there is no certainty of outcome but the continued struggle.

I didn't know it just then, but Europe was also a prelude to hearing my father's voice speak of home and away, and war and peace.

The letters that I received from my dad's family after my European trip gave me some further facts and insights into the Navigator's final few months on earth.

August 28, 1943, Lieutenant McGuire wrote to his brother Jack, a priest assigned to a parish in Garden City, Long Island:

As these things turn out, it now looks like we won't leave here until the 15th of the month or thereabouts, but even that is not certain, in fact nothing is certain in the Second Air Force (Force is often pronounced in the Bostonian fashion.)

They manage to keep us pretty busy out here what with ground school, Link Trainer, Bomb Trainer, gunnery, and - oh, yes - flying. We are scheduled to fly practically 12 out of every 24 hours. We fly six and are off 12 and that goes on until we have flown four shifts (Midnight to 6:00 am, 6:00 am to noon, noon to 6:00 pm, 6:00 pm to Midnight) and then we are given a 24 hour pass; and then the cycle starts over once again. It sounds like we get plenty of time in the air, but the way it usually works out due to the deplorable condition of the two planes our squadron possesses is that we are lucky to fly two shifts out of every four scheduled. A squadron, or at least our squadron has 18 crews. Can you imagine trying to prepare 18 crews for combat with two planes which are used 24 hours a day! It isn't even funny. I have flown exactly one mission long enough to do any navigation on and that was only about 700 miles. I'm not griping ...

By the way, I am flying B24's which are damn good airplanes with longer range and more speed than 17s

140

and the new 24G has as much fire power with its nose turret and belly turret.

The only ship I would rather fly in is a "29" which makes the 24 and 17 look like babies. If you ever see a ship with a long nose, 4 engines, a thin wing like the "24" and a single tail like the "17" but with a very high vertical fin, that will be a "29". I would like to tell you some of the things this ship is really capable of, Jack, but they are guarding its secrets so jealously that we can't even get close to the plane when one of them lands here. If it does half of what it is supposed to do, it will be a great additive factor in our winning the war quickly.

Muriel is writing to you today, so I guess she will give you all the local color and tell you about the average 105 degree temperature. I will have to sign off now since I am scheduled to fly in 15 minutes....we think of you often.

As ever,
Bill

11-29-43

Dear Mom and Dad:

Though the weather here is continuously damp and cold, the people, though very conservative and reserved, are on the whole very friendly, hospitable and open-hearted. They are willing to share most anything they have and they certainly haven't much of even what Americans consider every day fare, however. God bless America. There is no place like it in all the world, and the sooner I get 25 missions in and get home the happier I will be.

I haven't received any mail from home as yet, and I don't expect it will catch up to me until we are more settled than at present. Don't worry about me for I am fine, happy as I can be, in good health and still weigh about 180 - so you can see that we eat well at least. Say hello to all the McGuire tribe and all the gang for me. I think of you all very often. God bless you Mom and Dad.

All my love,
Bill

12-21-43

Dear Mom and Dad and Gang:

'Tis 4 days from the third successive Christmas I have been separated from you, Mom and Dad and the whole McGuire clan. I sure hope that this affair is well over and done with by Christmas of '44. I sure do miss Christmas at home. If the Army taught me nothing else, it has done a darn good job of putting across the fact that there is no place like home.

All my love to you and all
Your son, Bill

1-2-44

Dear Mom, Dad and gang:

Nothing much has happened here of late except the advent of a new year which brings with it the hope of a quick victory, and things are beginning to look rather good though most of the real hard work still lies ahead. Our boys and the RAF are doing a wonderful job of pasting the Reich's industry and are getting such good protective cover from the 38s, 47s, 51s and Spits that

losses in bombers are getting smaller each day we go
out. Our crew hasn't been on any missions over Germany
yet, but we are hoping to get in a lick or two pretty soon;
not so much because I am eager to get in the fight, but
more because I feel that the sooner will a distasteful job
be over and well consummated. Then we will all be able
to concentrate on the Japs in the Pacific. And when that
is done, turn our faces homeward and take up our normal
lives evermore. And I do believe I will be carrying Billy
on my shoulders to see his Grandma and Grandpa.

All my love, Bill

Brother Gerry in the following is the youngest member of the
family.

1-22-44

Dear Gerry:

It took your letter just one month to reach me. You
mailed it on the 22ⁿᵈ of Dec. and I received it tonight. I
was very glad to hear from you and especially glad to
hear that you gave those firemen so much help in putting
out that fire on Staten Island.

The cost of living must be rising by leaps and bounds
back home when you have to pay $10.00 for a pound of
bacon and four packs of cigarettes. I suppose you will
soon be paying a dollar apiece for hamburgers - though
there are plenty of fellows over here who'd gladly pay
that just to smell hamburger.

If you could come over here and go on a few rides
with us, you'd be a whiz when you returned to school,
especially in Geography, for the map of Europe just
unfolds under us each time we go up. At times it is lots of
fun Gerry, but it too, is awfully sad because you can't

help but realize that all the destruction and suffering of the people all over Europe was due to Hitler's mistaken conviction about Might making Right.

Always remember Ger, it is Right that makes Might.

Love - Bill

2-20-1944

Dear Jack:

Greetings from your brother, the one who writes so infrequently - now trying to compose a few words in the babble and din of the combat officers club of the 392ⁿᵈ somewhere in England. The fellows just returned from a trip and are rehashing it for the (censored) time - something like the way a Dodger fan dissects a game with the Giants over a beer in the neighborhood beer garden.

Our crew is due for a rest after tomorrow's mission (if there is one). We are getting a leave for about 10 days in which I intend to get down to southwestern England for a (censored) days of sun. The Gulfstream is supposed to hit the coast down there and make it a veritable tropics - at least as warm as Florida when it is not snowing. Then perhaps I'll spend a few days looking up old friends like Tom Walsh, Bill McLaughlin, Pat Muldowney and Ed Shanahan, a fellow navigator and classmate all through cadet training. Then back again to the usual humdrum business of combat life.

I put that rather poorly because I don't mean the missions are humdrum, but since we only fly perhaps one day out of every four and haven't much to do in between times, and few facilities for entertainment, life gets rather monotonous, being reduced mostly to sleeping, eating, writing letters and walking back and forth from barracks to mess hall.

As far as the actual missions go, they at best provide me with a lot of answers to Bill Jr.'s future questions on European geography. So far we have gone on (censored) missions and are still all in one piece with no resemblance whatsoever to Swiss cheese. Of course, we have picked up a few "flak" holes because the Heinies have developed quite a talent with their anti-aircraft guns. They just throw up a wall or rather a network of exploding steel fragments through which we must pass to get to the target. When a shell explodes within range of the plane, the fragments hitting the plane sound like hail on the roof of a Nissen hut, said roof being made of Galvanized iron. At times like this, we cross our fingers figuratively and hope nobody gets in the way of the pieces.

We don't worry too much about enemy fighters because we can shoot back at them, and more so because we usually have an escort of 47s, 51s, and 38s which are really better planes than anything the Germans can put up - though the Focke Wulf 190 is a hell of a good airplane and causes us lots of trouble.

The tempo is daily increasing in this Theater, Jack, and we are looking for the second front to be launched with the arrival of suitable weather, though truthfully, when and where it will be launched is as much a question to us as it is to you. True, we see the war actually going on but trying to predict coming events is like some person who reads the Home Talk (local news) trying to analyze Russian geopolitics ...

However, I do think the war in this Theater will be over before the football season rolls around again, and that will be mainly to keep the Russians out of Germany. With a little luck, I expect to be home by Labor Day myself, because as things stand now we only have to fly 25 missions over enemy territory before we are relieved from combat duty.

... I expect the combat tour may be lengthened as the war becomes more intense, or else we may be reassigned as instructors for a month or two before being sent home.

Well, Jack, I think I have bent your ear enough for one sitting so I'll close this letter soon, in fact just as soon as I've expressed the hope that God will keep you well and happy and that I will see you soon ...

As ever, Bill

3-6-44

Dear Dad:

By writing this letter today, I figure there is a faint possibility that you may receive it sometime within the next sixteen days. Anyway, "Happy Birthday, Dad and may you enjoy many more of them to come."

Remember the days quite a while ago when you used to call me Kaiser Bill. I used to take longer to walk past an ice cream parlor than any other store on the block. I am just waiting to see if Bill Jr. will try the same dodges with me as I use to try with you and Mom to get my own way. I wish I was home so that we could step out together and celebrate your birthday. Since I cannot be there, will you hold on to your raincheck until sometime in the summer when, God willing, I'll be home and take you and

Mom out to a dinner and all the fixings. Maybe we might even let mom have a Scotch and soda in honor of the occasion.

Things are rolling along over here increasing the tempo each day. The invasion might come off any day and then maybe it won't even be until months from now.

It looks to me as if we are concentrating on knocking the Luftwaffe out of the sky so that the odds will be that much less when our boys do land on the Continent. Jerry is trying desperately to conserve his fighter planes but he can't let us drop bombs every day without putting at least a semblance of defense up. The German people would probably revolt if they saw that their airforce wasn't trying to prevent their cities from being bombed.

So they compromise: one day they will put up a tremendous force of fighters to keep us from our objective, and the next day they will only have a few fighters opposing us. As you can see in the paper practically all our bombs of late have been aimed at airplane factories, and manufacturers of component parts of airplanes; and I think we are slowly succeeding in destroying the Germans only means of replenishing their diminishing supply of planes. The war will never be won from the air alone, but it is always a nice feeling to have Lefty Gomez pitching for your side.

By the way, it isn't a very nice feeling to be in a place that is being bombed. A little while back, I was in London during an air raid by Jerry. I had been to a movie and didn't even know there was an air raid going on. I walked a few blocks to a hotel wondering why the A-A-guns were doing so much firing. About 15 minutes later I was at the American Bar of the Ritz Hotel on Picadilly having a drink when I heard a terrific "boom" and the building shook and the lights went off for about a minute.

I found out later that the bomb had landed in the very street I had walked down 15 minutes before it had been dropped. Who says I haven't got a good Guardian Angel.

Well, I guess that is about all for now. Oh yes, I've been on 10 missions now, and none of our crew has been scratched - Thank God. Once again, "Happy Birthday" Dad. Give my love to all the gang. I miss them all!

As ever,

Bill

The Navigator's son considered himself fortunate. Not only did the European trip come to me essentially as a gift, giving me the impetus to do what otherwise may have seemed a little reckless, but I also kept making connections. I realized that many people who look for their links to the past often run into blind alleys and dead ends, and once located, non-cooperation from people in a position to help.

The only personal frustration I felt was an odd sense of alienation at the center of the experience. For one thing, no matter how often I told the story of my research or how well, my own passion did not seem to translate to my listeners. People did listen and they said the right things. They were positive in their responses, even glad for me. It was simply that there was something missing. I could see it in their eyes. And it wasn't a lack of empathy, and the length and strength of my relationship to them didn't have any bearing. Even with family, I had flashes of that uncertainty or disappointment in their reaction.

I didn't know why. I didn't know what it was precisely that was out of sync. But it was there. To me, everything that had happened was good news. Something positive in life that deserved to be shared. So I kept on preaching the good news. But I also resigned myself to the fact that my voyage of discovery about my father was so deeply personal and many layered for me, that in some respects it was beyond telling, beyond sharing.

I realized too, that I was constantly running the risk of overplaying the experience. Certainly some strange things had happened, but they could all be explained by random chance and my own drive and near obsession to piece the story together and find out everything there was to find out. Yet I also believed that the life of the spirit continued. And as I had matured, in a way that other men come to respect or make peace with their fathers as they age, my conviction grew that the presence of my father had never been far from my life.

I had doubts the way any rational human being has about their closest beliefs. But I accepted my doubt as the price we pay for the privilege of believing. So I balanced all these feelings as I continued along the path I began in the fall of '93. I recognized the tale was coming to an end. I joked with my wife and children about going over the edge. And I searched on, eager to see where the Navigator would take me next.

That Labor Day weekend of '95, together with our two sons, Bernadette and I drove to the Marine Park section of Brooklyn and out to Floyd Bennett field on the Jamaica Bay end of Flatbush Avenue. A World War II air show was going on, which included a restored B17 and a B24 J, the All American. This would be our first encounter with the old Liberator. They were selling rides to the public but I didn't want to spend the money just then. I said to son Matt, "Maybe some other time. I'm not dead yet." But we were able to see the inside of the craft, along with hundreds of others who wiggled through the Lib's confining spaces. We took pictures and video tape and crawled all over the fuselage. We were not allowed into the nose, however, and had to content ourselves with peering down and in from the cockpit entrance.

Though the size of the ship was striking, we still came away with the strong sense of what tight quarters the ten-man crew worked in. And too, that it was a warship constructed with great cost and care to do a very specific job for a limited period of time. A lot of the interior looked rough and unfinished with bare wires hanging out, for example, probably for easy access. There were no cosmetics, just pure function. But here it was fifty years later and still operational. If in the end, the Liberators and Forts had been built to last, it was only because, in those days, virtually everything made in America was made to last. With rare exception, however, they were all converted into metal scrap in the years after the war. That was what made the All American and the few remaining ships like her so special.

I corresponded with Franz Helle now and then, encouraging him to pursue some local leads and to keep me informed of any further information. Franz sent a copy of reporter Marga Kohr's story from the town paper and I had it translated. Later, Marga herself sent another copy along with some original photographs she had taken. In January 1996, I received a letter from Franz with four rare sepia tinted photos. They were crash scene photos. Franz received them from a man named Herbert Griesbaum who once had lived near Ettenheimmunster. Evidently, Herbert had read of my visit in the newspaper.

I wrote to Griesbaum at the address Franz had included, asking for information about the circumstances of these pictures and if there were more.

Of the four, three seemed to be of the wreckage of Peterson's "Big Time Operator." None of the photos were particularly good or clear, but again they were documentary. The terrain around the first three was flat and open, while the fourth was obviously in heavy woods. There did not seem to be any evidence of a bad fire visible in any of the photos. If guards were meant to keep the local people away, that was not apparent here. In one shot, a young man holds one of the plane's sixty-five-pound 50-caliber machine guns.

I put the photos carefully away. It would be several weeks before I realized, going over them again with a magnifying glass, that the one in the trees, with a young boy standing on the wreckage, was of the "Sinister Minister." For there under the circle D insignia on the tail were the numbers 100117.

I had copies made and sent them to Cliff Peterson and his friend and former engineer, Malcolm Hinshaw.

In March, I finally linked up with Jim Marsteller for the first time. Jim had been my first information source in '93 and was the nephew of another 392nd airman killed March 18, 1944. Together with his cousin Jim Morris, we went to check out the Missing Air Crew Report files at the National Archives, recently relocated to spiffy new quarters in College Park, Maryland. I was amazed at the numbers of people sitting there researching away on a weekday. We checked, at Marsteller's urging, not only the translated captured documents but also the files of original German papers but didn't really come up with anything new.

I did find a list of all downed American planes for March and April 1944 which identified from where and from what units the lost bombers had come. I raced through this list from front to back, and back to front again, hoping to identify the third craft that had crashed at Ettenheimmunster. Then I realized that two pages were missing and they were the sheets I needed.

Jim Morris took a tripod time-release photo of the three of us outside the archive. The two Jims drove me to my hotel where we had a few brewskis and talked about our overall research successes and the mutually disappointing day. Then they left me to return to Pennsylvania.

In addition to trying to identify the remaining plane and its crew, I had also been hopeful I could learn more about the specific resting places of the American airmen who had died at Ettenheimmunster.

From the German and American records, it was clear that eleven American airmen, probably all from the two Liberators, had been laid to rest in the village's new cemetery. Ten initially, and Masters later the same summer. The records placed Masters in the first grave position followed by Jimmie Byrd and Ora Harrell from the Peterson plane. In the last three graves were Leon Hancock, from Peterson's crew, flanked by Lt. McGuire and N. Maylander from #117. It seemed from the documents that the rest of the graves were occupied only by members of those two same crews.

What wasn't clear early on was whether the Germans were speaking of #117 or Peterson's #981 when they noted removing one unburned body to Lahr for burial. This corresponded with the fact that there remained five of eleven graves whose occupants are undetermined from the documents. But there were six dead remaining from the two airplanes: E. Brown, F. Wallace, W. Sharpe, N. Bandura, R. Huffman and F. Richardson. In all probability, one of Sharpe's #117 crew was the exception buried at Lahr. There were no clues, however, at the National Archives that could be accessed that March day.

As for the third wrecked plane, I only came across information already in my possession. First the Germans described it as possibly a British Lancaster or an American Pathfinder. Pathfinders had special radar equipment on their bellies that allowed them, in theory, to lead the other bombers to a target despite cloud cover or other bad conditions. But in the later German documents the site #3 wreck was described as a Fortress II, a B17, with "Signs: K - on the side - wing J." This sketchy, annoyingly ambiguous description was all I had to go on. Nonetheless, the "J" would later prove significant.

The next day, Saturday, March 16, I was scheduled to be at Uncle Gerry McGuire's place in Alexandria, Virginia, in the late afternoon. Prompted by my unexpected phone call that morning, my aunt and uncle invited their surprise guest to have dinner and spend the night. In the late morning, after my phone call, I visited the Holocaust Museum in D.C. for the first time and spent five hours there. Of all the searing sights and words I took in there, the moments I spent alone in the barren freight car outside the reconstructed main gate to Auschwitz formed an indelible image in my mind.

Later, just before dinner, Gerry gave me a small bundle of dad's letters that he had been holding since my grandmother passed away, including the original of the V mail letter Gerry himself had received from the Navigator early in 1944. He also gave me my father's maroon block "B" varsity letter from Brooklyn College.

It was then that I spoke of the question that had been on my mind for some time but had previously gone unspoken. Did my father ever see me? Did father and son ever meet?

They didn't know. Marilyn said: "I don't know any facts one way or the other. I was just a girl then. But I can tell you I'm sure the two of you were together."

I slept in a basement room and flipped on the TV to find college basketball playoff scores. Roaming around the channels at about 11 p.m., I came across an extreme close-up of the hero of the *Magnum P. I.* series, as he apparently sat alone, in a chair in his apartment, watching television. His expression was grave, but thoughtful. I was frozen by this for a minute or two, as all that could be heard was the audio from the TV within the drama. An off-camera voice said, "They'll never make it to Friedrichshafen. They'll never get out of the forest."

Credits came up. The scene changed. There was no further reference to this except the story then seemed to deal with American prisoner of war experiences in Vietnam. This puzzled me that night as I tried to sleep and all the way home on Amtrak. When I had told my uncle about it over breakfast, Gerry had whistled the music from *The Twilight Zone.*

By Tuesday, I had tracked down the producer. To the best of his knowledge, according to the fax he sent me, the source of that fragment of dialogue was the motion picture *Stalag 17.* He admitted no special connection to Friedrichshafen or the Eighth Air Force. It was just a coincidence. One that happened within hours of the 52nd anniversary of the mission!

One evening some months after my trip to D.C., I met an old friend for drinks on my way to the train home. He was in town from his new base in Chicago and as we caught up with each other, I filled him in on the story of retracing my father. He was particularly interested in the letters I had received and after some time confessed that he too, was in possession of a cache of letters of somewhat similar circumstances.

He spoke of a young nephew, of the boy's mother, my friend's sister and of her marriage to a nineteen-year-old youngster on the eve of a combat infantry tour in Vietnam. The young soldier was killed and the sister had his son. Somehow, my friend ended up with the soldier's letters home to his young wife. She had had her problems since then and so had her son, in terms of adjusting to the world. The letters were not particularly flattering according to the story teller. They provided little insight into the character of the deceased except perhaps to reveal a certain immaturity.

My companion wondered out loud if he should give his young nephew the letters his father had sent home. What was to be gained? He didn't have the slightest idea if the youngster would even have an interest in them. Yet, he had carefully held onto them and now he asked me the question.

In response, I told him what my experience had taught me. It is always better to know, even if these letters revealed very little, or said nothing truly positive. Even if the young man had a negative or an indifferent reaction to what his father had recorded, the letters were a concrete connection to his past, I said. I think I only told my old buddy what he already knew, that when you come down to it, this is something the survivors deserve to have put before them to handle and dispose of as they see fit. For better or for worse.

In 1994, when I had met Jack Olsen, that old navigator friend of my dad's, for lunch at Sardi's in New York City, there was a lull in the conversation after our initial exchange. I then said to him, hoping to get him to warm to the subject and to reveal a little more, "Well tell me, what kind of man was my father, what stands out in your mind?" He looked up from his food and with a curiously cold stare said, "I just told you, didn't I?"

Remembering my life as a youngster I suppose it was easy even for me to rationalize why people who knew both me and my dad were so unwilling to tell me anything about him. There was my mother's strong opposition, and there was the fact of her remarriage and her husband's attitudes about my dad. Whether actively or passively, my stepfather must have viewed my father and his memory as an interloping presence in our life as a family.

But the reluctance of aunts, uncles, grandparents and some of dad's old friends to fill in the blanks in my young life seemed to go beyond that. As I got older, and even after my mom's death, that really didn't change for the most part. Maybe they read too much into the situation. Or perhaps, I thought, they just didn't feel there was very much to share with me that I would want to hear. I believe people are generally reluctant to deal with anything of a truly personal nature. It was also true that my contacts with the older generation of relatives became, over time, more infrequent and as a result, more awkward. Finally, those who knew and remembered "the boy" now saw me as a man with a life of my own and assumed I had moved well past the wounds of childhood.

I did, however, continue to wonder about these things, and particularly my mother, and just what she thought to accomplish by her silence. This aspect of our relationship was consistent with the desperate way she had tried to deny certain things and patch our life together. She could never view her efforts to control me and my life as a disservice to me, for she always thought of me as an extension of herself. In the end that illusion would desert her as well, though we remained tied by stronger bonds and still do.

So for me, there were no letters home to inherit from my mom, just the ones dad sent to his own family. When I got home from Alexandria I shared these with my wife and daughter. Molly was amazed by the striking similarity of my father's handwriting to mine. So was Bernadette. I thought my penmanship was chicken scratch next to his. But I was struck by the familiarity of much of the style, language, and voice in my father's letters. It was almost as if I had manufactured the text myself. Maybe I was just tricking myself or, more likely, the fact that the two of us had some of the same wiring meant that we approached a blank page in much the same fashion.

My weekend in Washington and all that transpired had also rekindled the memory of a family trip we took there in the early 1990s for a wedding. That Sunday, the six of us had gone out to Arlington Cemetery in unbearable June heat and humidity. We watched the changing of the guard at the Tomb of the Unknown Soldier, while the sweat rolling down the faces of the rigid soldiers matched that of all the spectators. Then we visited the Lincoln Monument and, for the first time, the Vietnam Memorial.

I lost friends in 'Nam. Some, kids I had known in high school, I didn't learn about until much later. But there are two young men I think of very often, and still see so clearly in my mind's eye, just as I last left them. One was a college national track star. A terrific, happy, tough, engaging guy who lived as if there were a thousand lifetimes bottled up in his lean athletic frame. He wasn't supposed to because of the risk of injury, but he was a regular for our dormitory pick-up half-court basketball games. He was an IC4A champion in his senior year. He left a beautiful young wife and children behind.

The second was a younger brother of my best man. A tall, gangling, serious kid, full of promise, who couldn't help but reveal some of his inner goodness in a sudden, bashfully reluctant smile. A great student, solid, capable, from the best stock.

They were here. Then over there. And then both of them were gone, wiped away. One black. One white. All-American.

With my children, I found both their names on the black marble memorial wall.

I still have my draft card. Over "date of mailing" it is stamped December 14, 1965, in purple ink. It is signed by Jack Daniels, no relation, I supposed, to the Tennessee sour mash people. The type next to "Class" reads 4A.

My wife was expecting our first child then. My mother was overwrought about any chance of my being inducted. But President Truman had signed a public law in his first term that excused from service the sole surviving children of the WWII deceased. I was deferred because of my father. Back then I was fairly cavalier about it all. Looking back today I have no doubt that it probably saved my life.

Just a feeling, like the feeling I have for my two dead friends. As I located their names on the wall, my daughter said that she would go and get a volunteer so I could make tracings. "No," I said, reaching up. "It will be enough just to touch them."

And it was.

As the winter wound down, I continued to worry over the unknown plane at Ettenheimmunster. Bernadette had given me two valuable textbooks by Roger A. Freeman: *The Mighty Eighth* and *The Mighty Eighth War Diary* that were definitive summaries of the units and battles of the WWII campaign. The letter "J" was the one concrete piece of evidence that the Germans had put on the record. Now, checking through the illustrations, I saw several units that used a "J" as a principal marking in March 1944. One of these was the 390th Bomb Group, where my contact John Warner had already provided invaluable service.

Looking over the history of the 390th on March 18, 1944, in the same references, I saw that they had flown a mission that same day to Augsburg. Furthermore, they had lost one bomber. I wrote to John Warner at the 390th library in Arizona, enclosing the documents and information I had, including the names of three possible survivors from the mystery plane.

About May 1, I received Warner's reply: "It seems clear that your listing of the crew of the crashed aircraft on 18 March 1944 was a 390th, A/C #42-37925. See the enclosed copy of page 41 from our "History of Aircraft Assigned" and copies of the relevant documents from our records." What followed was the name and address of a survivor and active member of the association, Harry Houck of West Virginia, and a second revelation.

Number 925 was piloted by Robert "Wade" Biesecker and they were on their twenty-third mission. Their regular navigator C.C. Marshall finished his tour on March 16 and was replaced on the 18th by a man named Irving M. Nordendahl. I also saw on the attached crew list that the name of one of the regular waist gunners on #925 was F. Grover Wallace. **There were two Wallaces** on two different planes that crashed in the vicinity of Ettenheimmunster that same March day. Frank Wallace, the #117 radio operator died aboard the "Sinister Minister". F. Grover Wallace got out and, after recovering in German hospitals, survived the war.

I gave myself a good whack in the head. But who would have thought such a thing possible? In the one or two places it had appeared in the captured documents, I had attributed the name "Grover" or "Crover" Wallace to an error. I put the different serial number down to the same reason. But the Germans hadn't been guilty of sloppy work, I had been.

Earlier, Franz had sent me still another deposition from 1945, untranslated. It was taken from the mayor of Wallburg and dealt with the discovery of the #925 crew, their burial at Lahr, and the later discovery and burial of Lt. Wade Biesecker at Wallburg. I didn't attach any particular significance to this German document, but when I received a second copy that spring, I finally had it translated with some others. Six bodies had been placed in coffins and, after a time in Wallburg, shipped to Lahr, the mayor had said. "When the rescue squad began to dismantle (salvage) the plane and carry away parts that could still be used, the remains of another dead person were found under some wreckage lying in the woods of Ettenheim forest." The pilot was buried in the local cemetery March 23, the document said. They said a brief eulogy and laid a memorial wreath at the grave. "The name of this dead man (Lieutenant Biesecker) is recorded in the local directory of graves."

More details came from Harry Houck, the radio operator, whom I first contacted within a week of learning his name and number. They were hit on the way back from bombing a Messerschmitt factory at about 2 p.m., he guessed. But it could have been later. Formation was broken up by fighter attacks and the left side engine closest to his radio work station was shot off, with the second engine there also on fire. They were being attacked by three ME 109s. The bail out signal was given and Houck said he was supposed to be the fifth man out. With the signal, he was expected to report to the pilot that the back of the plane was empty and then go. But he said, "None of them had got out yet." Then he jumped. He didn't really see anything or hear anything after that but thinks pieces of the plane may have come down past him.

Houck said Wallace, from a small town near Lima, Ohio, broke his back as he came down in a tree. Wallace spent virtually the rest of the war in German hospitals but recovered and became a machinist back in the States. The two vets met up in Miami back in 1945, while undergoing R and R, rest and rehabilitation. Houck said Wallace called him religiously every March 18 after that. Recently, Grover Wallace passed away. There was one other survivor, Michael Farrowich, from Brooklyn, N.Y. But Harry said Farrowich had relocated and left no forwarding address. Houck was open, genial, and glad to hear from me. He explained that he is a retired railroad brakeman and conductor, who now operates a hardware store and loves it. He is a grandfather, and had suffered no injuries in getting out of #925. He invited me to drop by when I was in his neck of the woods.

I was quietly elated about identifying the third plane at Ettenheimmunster and detailing its fate. It was one contribution to this account that I made solely on my own, as the result of intuition, some detective work, and a bit of luck. Now, anything seemed possible.

Herbert Griesbaum in Germany eventually responded to my earlier inquiry. He sent me three additional crash site photos that were not very good but indicated quite a few people milling about the wreckage. Herbert gave his account of the solo German fighter shooting down the three bombers and told of how he and his schoolboy friends had come to take the photos. There were no more, he added.

Was the March 18 attack on Friedrichshafen successful? Like the ultimate effect of the heavy bombing campaign against Germany itself, the question remains open to some debate. Colonel Myron Keilman, who led the 392nd's worst mission, said what may be his final word on that subject in a newsletter article he wrote some years ago. One of the veterans sent a copy to me. The summary concluded: "The consoling afterthoughts of the 392nd's most disastrous mission are that several of the Second Air Division's B24 bombardment groups made devastating hits on the primary objective, and Friedrichshafen was never rescheduled as a target."

As it turned out the Army Air Forces did return to the target after all. Jim Marsteller shared a letter with me that he had received from a Dr. George Wieland on "Stadt Friedrichshafen" letterhead inviting Jim to join a number of USAAF vets of raids on the city for a commemorative seminar there around the fiftieth anniversary. The series of exhibits and events, including academics and ex-German military personnel, stretched from March to November 1994. "An excursion" to a local V2 rocket site was included in the package of activities.

The official's letter read in part: "We received the letters and enclosures several weeks later and were very pleased with the communicated recollections, partly combined with copies of war diaries. Most of the information concerned the raids of March 16 and 18, some the raid of April 24, 1944. There was no information about the Eighth Air Force raid of February 25, 1945, and the sorties of the 15th Air Force (July 18 and 20, August 3 and 16, 1944)."

The United States Strategic Bombing Survey, January, 1947 for "Dornier Works Friedrichshafen and Munich Germany," accessed at the Pentagon library, indicates that from 1943 until the end of the war that there were seven American attacks on the Friedrichshafen plants and nine attacks on the Munich Dornier facilities. The survey reports that results are inconclusive, due to speedy recovery programs and the German strategy of "disbursement" or deconcentration and relocation of facilities. But there was significant damage and production delay with each raid, and the Dornier experimental tandem bomber, the DO-335, as a result of the repeated bombing, never approached full production and was not a factor in the war.

What did come across loud and clear in my research was that Friedrichshafen was one of the most important missions of the war. Author-historian Len Deighton wrote to me, for example: "F'hafen was considered 'a target of prime strategic, operational and tactical significance' because there were engine factories and other war plants too. Where the old Zeppelin works once stood there was a plant producing sophisticated radar, including radar installations fitted to night fighters. Anthony Verrier's well respected book *The Bomber Offensive* says F'hafen was arguably of greater importance than the Ruhr Dams which RAF Bomber Command sacrificed so much to attack."

In the beginning of May 1996 I had a business trip to Orlando, Florida, for a meeting. I took an extra day and drove up to visit Mr. and Mrs. Cliff Peterson at their home in Winter Park. We had a good dinner in town and then sat and talked. Cliff supplied a lot of valuable detail, as had his crewmate, Malcolm Hinshaw, through the mail. Towards the end of my visit, Cliff spoke somewhat reluctantly about his wounds. And, of his liberation at Moosburg, where virtually all the imprisoned Allied fliers had been congregated by April '45 by the Nazis. None of them knew exactly why. But Patton's Army got to them and freed them. And Cliff realized, one good morning, that he was staring at the red, white, and blue flag of his country flapping above the camp. Then the tears and the recognition that the ordeal was over came at the same time to this gentleman, who would later serve his country once again with distinction in Korea.

I was glad I finally met the survivor, and there is a photo of the two of us arm and arm on a fine May day.

For me, Peterson epitomized the best of the men of the Eighth Air Force and qualities I saw in so many remaining veterans of the great global conflict. On the surface they led routine lives and coped with all the challenges of senior citizenship at the twilight of the twentieth century. But under that mundane cover shone a quiet confidence and a moral seriousness that they could not free themselves from even if they chose. They all had it, a call to true leadership. And they shared a vision, an enduring memory of brotherhood in the face of death and apocalyptic evil. That brotherhood lives for them still.

At the beginning, when Mike Cugini had called 1943-44 the best time in his life, I was genuinely puzzled. How could that be? Certainly surviving was a supreme moment to relish. Going home. Building a career and a family. The restaurant business for the Cuginis, being very much part of the life of their hometown community for so many years. But no, "the best" was being with the crew of #117.

What Mike expressed was what I saw too in Cliff Peterson and picked up on again and again in conversations with the old airmen. What it was was a sense of finely tuned purpose, of resolve, a fire that then had burned bright with all the passion of their youth. In brotherhood, they knew what they had to do. They stayed the course, clinging desperately to each other and their sanity in the face of a deadening daily routine. And for a while, that flame was the light of the world. I could catch it still, see it flash even now in their gaze. Mike Cugini had gotten it right after all. Despite all the blood and the cruel loss, you could begin to see it was the best time of their lives.

And, of course, it had been the worst time of their lives as well. I did get to go to a reunion of the Eighth airmen, in St. Paul, Minnesota, and met some of the 392nd men who served with my dad. While I was with them, I was struck by the bonds between us, the vets of WWII and people like me, children of the war deceased. We all led two lives, the workaday outward existence and an internal life as well, a life back there, a life of remembrance and reaching for something never quite within our grasp.

At times they reveal this conflict and show their inner feelings, the trauma of a never healing wound. And, at times, they shy away from revealing anything, hiding from the hold of the war in the underpinnings of whom they had become. Anything but experiencing that terrible frightening vulnerability once more. It was as if their skin might suddenly be peeled back like the thin outer casing of that aluminum craft they once inhabited and they would find themselves trapped again. Exposed, for fate to decide once more who would suffer and perish and who might come through. And it would be no consolation to have to let go of a brother's hand, to release its already cold grip to rejoin the world of the living. The survivors are on both sides of that uncertain line, always.

And how alike we are, we too, who show ourselves and hide, pretending we don't see the beast over our shoulder. The grinning beast of death and disorder in a swastika armband. And oh, see what a familiar face it has, a human face. It mocks and sneers on dancing feet and our choking fear is that it may laugh at us through all of eternity. It was all for nothing, the beast roars. For nothing!

What odd bodies we are as well, in a world gone way beyond materialism, proud that it has outgrown so many of the values that were not so long ago held to be the core of community and humanity. A world where the notion that anything might be worth dying for is viewed as backward and uninformed. The old warriors and the aging children of the dead, we seem sometimes like dusty curios on the shelf of a faded shop in a town where everyone moved away when they built the new Interstate.

At the reunion's final breakfast, I confessed to Cliff Peterson's wife, Mary, that I had doubts that my story would ever find its way into print. She looked straight at me and said, matter of factly: "Well, you should just keep on trying, shouldn't you." A little while later, the meeting closed with a beautiful but simple memorial ceremony for the dead of the Eighth Air Force. As each group, all the outfits, were called off in the makeshift chapel in the hotel ballroom, their representatives walked down the center aisle with a long stem rose and placed them, side by side, on the head table. I carried a flower for my father and his group and placed it in the middle of the long, long red row. Then came the haunting notes of *Taps*.

No, some things you don't forget. Some things are worth dying for. I was with people who understood, and both glad and grateful to be in their company. This time it was the beast who was doing the hiding.

At the very beginning of October 1996, I received a letter from Franz Helle in Ettenheimmunster with a copy of an old document enclosed. As a result of his own research with the Militararchiv Freiburg, Franz had evidence for the first time that identified the dark, curly haired young man who had been removed from the rest of the dead of #117, "Sinister Minister." Frank Richardson, the bombardier, was buried along with the other six from Houck's B17 at Lahr by the Luftwaffe.

Just about all the questions and puzzles were solved.

There was some contradictory evidence about how many planes the 392nd put up March 18, 1944, when the aborts took place, and the nature of the formations. But ultimately I was confident in the mission file evidence and official records of the 392nd. It all supported my understanding of what had happened, free of any apparent exception.

Tom McConnell, a local acquaintance and former Lib bombardier with the 15th Air Force in Italy, took issue with Mike

Cugini's bail out story as I had told it to him. This vet said there was no way anyone could run around without their high altitude boots above 20,000 feet without severe frostbite in a matter of minutes. His conjecture: unzipped boots often came off when the parachute jerked open, and Cugini, in the bewildering pressure of those moments, simply had a confused memory of the actual sequence of events.

Eventually, through my contacts with the 392nd BG Memorial Association, I was put in touch with two more vets who were friends of my dad's and had served with him at Wendling. Ken Parks of McFarland, Wisconsin, went through navigation school and training with Lt. McGuire. He sent me a crisp new $10 bill to replace the British £5 note he borrowed from my dad the winter of '44 for a stake in a poker game. It was Parks who told me about the Catholic chaplain oversleeping the morning of March 18. Ken was interned in Switzerland with the balance of the Haffermehl crew after their ship crash landed and burned in a freshly plowed field. This was "The Arsenal," or as Ken preferred to call it, "Late Date II", #826. In late '44, he escaped with some other airmen, joining up with our final offensive. He was then sent home.

Howard Bjork, of Amarillo, Texas, the regular bombardier on the Feran crew, was in hospital on March 18, 1944, when his plane and Dalton's collided, killing all but one. He too, went through training with Lt. McGuire at: Clovis, New Mexico; Pueblo, Colorado; Salina and Topeka, Kansas. He said for most of them the next stop was Camp Shanks, Nyack, New York, and it was possible the Sharpe crew came in later. He recalled that my dad and he left New York on the *Queen Elizabeth* the first week in November. "We landed at Greenock, Scotland, in the Firth of Clyde on November 9, 1943, and spent the first few nights in a barracks in a place called Troon." Then it was England, classes, and some flying from Stoke-on-Trent, Cheddington, and Attlebridge. "We were assigned to the 392nd in December 1943," he added. Howard Bjork told me of visiting with my mom and grandparents in late '44 while he was recovering from his severe injuries. He was also the source of the personal info about John Feran. Howard concluded, "I liked Bill, I guess everybody did."

Harry Houck, the radio man on the B17 downed at Ettenheimmunster, secured the 390th's mission file for their March 18, 1944 trip to Augsburg and shared it with me. It pinpointed the time of the fatal attack "by six ME 109s" to 1520 hours, the same approximate time the 392nd lost the Cliff Peterson and Bill Sharpe Liberators at roughly the same location. According to depositions of two of the survivors, the remaining crew, except for the officers in the nose, had been gathered at the main hatch and were ready to jump when the plane exploded. Harry did learn one new fact: T/Sgt. Peter Repka, the top turret gunner, was credited with shooting down an ME 109 on the mission.

Jim Marsteller made a second visit to Germany in the fall of 1996. He discovered more evidence and wreckage from March 18, 1944 and interviewed many eyewitnesses. He also eventually found Chester Strickler's young friend with the fondness for chewing gum, now a resident of the U.S.A. This man's version of events was different from Strickler's recollection. More than one side to every story, I said. There always seemed to be more to learn and Jim kept at it.

For the Navigator's son, the unfinished business that remained was close at hand. Mike Cugini had asked me with real emotion if I knew what became of young Bill McGowan, their regular belly gunner on #117. On the day of the mission, Covenez had been his replacement. I said I didn't know anything about the man they had all thought of as their lucky mascot. But one day, looking over the list of 392nd dead at St. Avold, I noticed the answer had been staring me in the face all along. Just above my father's name was that of William J. McGowan, S.Sgt., 579th of New York. Killed April 11, 1944. Billy had escaped Friedrichshafen only to be shot down over Bernberg less than a month later.

Together, father, mother, and son. It was a reasonable assumption that this scenario took place but I could only guess. No one ever told me and I honestly don't remember if I ever asked. There hadn't been much opportunity between my birth in April 1943 and my father's overseas departure in the fall, probably around Halloween. One of the striking bits of information I had collected was an old newspaper clipping with a large photo of the *Queen Mary* steaming up the Narrows into New York Bay. The June 21, 1945, article, in the short-lived daily *PM,* said that the great ship had arrived the previous day on its first New York cruise since VE Day. Among the 14,526 returning servicemen and women, "the first and liveliest troops to debark were the members of the 392nd Bomb. Group."

"Two yachts carrying Army bands and the cutter *Sandy Hook*, a former excursion boat, carrying reporters and cameramen, met her at the Narrows and escorted her through a harbor full of welcoming vessels, all sounding the traditional three-whistle salute of welcome. A tug attempted a bugle call on its whistle; a huge sign on the green embankment before Fort Hamilton said: 'Welcome Home - Well Done'… Army piers were decorated in red, white, and blue; crowds lined the Bay Ridge waterfront." High above, a Navy dirigible dutifully trailed the battleship-gray painted steamer, while alongside the *Queen*, New York City's *The Firefighter,* the most powerful fireboat in the world, gushed 20,000 gallons a minute in its own geyser-like salute. From all along the shorelines, and on Staten Island ferries, aircraft carriers, and boats of every description, the crowds kept waving and calling out. Their delirious shouts blended with the band music and boat horns in one sustained tumultuous roar. And through it all, Lady Liberty, her torch held high, continued her watch. Her gaze extended past Gravesend, far out to sea.

When I was a toddler, I remember being taken to the nearby Brooklyn-Narrows shoreline to watch the great naval ships and carriers come home, blue fighters on deck with folded wings. Reading the *PM* article it wasn't hard to imagine a different outcome when my mother, too, may have stood on the crest of that tree-shaded hill in Owl's Head Park with me in her arms to cheer her husband home with the men of the 392nd. But it just wasn't meant to be.

Yet the heart goes on. In all humility, I have come to understand that the love my parents once shared lives in me. Despite everything that had happened to her, my mother loved me and taught me to love. When the chips are down, she taught me to go with the heart. Sometimes I may have stumbled and failed along the way, but I have tried to be a loving person, one who grows through love and dares to speak and act from the heart. The implications of this aspect of my nature are profound. I see them in my children, my grandchildren, in the very quality of their lives. It is a stubborn and beautiful heritage. In this line of continuity I can also see that, perhaps after all, the three of us, father, mother, and son, were on that hill together. To see our ship come in. My mother lives on for me, as my father lives. The heart does go on, and on.

After coming back from my visit to my uncle's place in Alexandria and noodling over it a while longer, I had written to one of my father's sisters, Rosemary, and asked the same question I had put to Gerry and Marilyn: had father and son ever met? Were the Navigator and the boy ever together?

Her reply came some time later. She spoke of her direct knowledge of those times and the last time she saw my father and heard from him. Then she zeroed in on my question. "I wasn't in New York at all for nearly two years but I talked with my sister, Dorothy, and asked her to go deep into her memory and to try to recall." She also called her sister Catherine on the same subject.

The picture my aunts painted was of a fine day, a carriage stroll to Grandma's house. My father and his officers met us on their way to ship out and he held me in his arms and proudly showed me off to the men of #117. Copilot Norb Bandura assured Bill's sister not to worry, they would take good care of Bill. They'd get him back. The other two voiced their agreement. It was all but done.

And at this instant, as I read the letter, I felt the same cool fleeting touch, on the back of my neck, of an open hand. The way you would hold the head of an infant to support it.

It wasn't a spook. There was no visitation. Rather, it was as if the imprint of my father's touch from so very long ago had registered in my young nervous system and now, like a scent from the past, it flooded my senses again and just as quickly left me. To me, this was no illusion or self-delusion. It was a clear tangible thing as real as pain or the difference between a conscious and unconscious state. It had simply happened.

A little while later, letter in hand, I told the story to my wife. She understood what I was telling her and was moved by it. It was a final link in the strange chain of events that had begun long before I started my search in 1993.

She sat by me and put her hand over mine. "Those young men on one-one-seven," I said to her. "They told my father's sister that day as he held me and showed me off. They told her they would get him back, would bring him home again. And you know babe, I believe in the end they kept their promise. Don't you?"

Epitaph
Standing Down/Final Grace

So why all this fuss and bother? A young man goes off to war, and leaving family behind, is slain. Like so many. An ordinary man in the end.

Yes, so many. And this war, war is abomination. Senseless killing, destruction, unspeakable horror in which none is true winner and all are marked by the stain.

But look into the hearts of men to know their motivation and to weigh their action. Who would condemn those who raise their arms to fend the innocent, and smite the enemy who would destroy all if he himself is not destroyed.

The Navigator was one of the thousands who volunteered to bring the war to Germany to stop the destruction and oppression. He was in that company of men who, with their fellow soldiers and allies, helped wipe out the Nazi power in the air and mortally crippled his war machine. The effort of the RAF and U.S. Air Forces in this crucial two years of battle made the invasion and sweep across France and Belgium possible and proved invaluable to the Russian advance in the east.

Will history continue to hold high the example of these men? Who will speak for them? Soon others will not be able to call on them any longer. It will be up to a new generation. Time is passing. The men of the Eighth are standing down. The last of the Liberators go to their rest.

Part of the answer lies here at the cemetery where the Navigator's son spoke to him. There are only the graves of ordinary men here at St. Avold. Ten thousand ordinary men. The field is lush green. Cumulus clouds gently push their way in the blue out across France and the dark Atlantic. A little bird alights on the head of the stone eagle that surveys the field of white monuments. Another rises from a tree and races with the clouds.

Ordinary men. There are many now who dismiss their efforts and those of the men who fought with them. But in this place, at St. Avold, there are no cynics, only believers. For each infantry man and airman who lies here chose to put his life on the line for a cherished belief. Ultimately. It was a time when men kept a pledge once given. It was a time for sacrifice.

In this way these men are not unlike those we passed on our journey to this place. For everywhere the Navigator's son went he encountered the blood of martyrs. Soldiers of a different kind. Avold himself, or Nabor, as he is also called. And Landelin, the Celt, who returned to the Rhineland where his own ancestors had begun more than a millennium before. Returned with the news of a new god, a caring god.

Martyrs! The word comes from the ancient Greek for witnesses. In this age even the churchmen are uncertain if many of these revered dead ever really existed. If they were ever more than the myths of the people, ordinary people, to sanctify their daily struggle and give some semblance of lasting meaning to humble lives. Legend.

But who can say what is the folly of men and what is the truth that goes beyond time?

And the clouds speed more rapidly now. And the sun sets and rises. Again, and more quickly. Time is racing, spinning by here. Days, months, years, centuries in a blinding fury. The gates of the cemetery fall, the crosses crumble or are swallowed in the changing contours of the earth shaped by snow, ice, rain, and wind. And the hand of man, the usurper. Encroachment is made on the field. Structures rise up and in time fall away. The spiraling sky of more than a millennium hence begins to slow once again. Now most of the cemetery is an open field once more. The horizon is settled, normal. It is a late spring day with the sun beginning to ease into the west. A bird lands on the branch of a tree and sounds his call. The raucous voices of children at play seem to answer.

They appear from over a rise above the field. A ragtag bunch of boys and girls, perhaps a dozen of them. All of young ages. One trips on a stone and curses. Then he comes back to the spot and digs his toes in the soil around a smooth angled piece of white marble. A second child with a stick joins the game of digging.

A tall young man of about fourteen years appears now at the top of the rise. He carries a staff that is bigger than he by several feet. Just below him yet another child rubs his hand against the eroding soil of the embankment and exclaims excitedly, "Here's one more." The others run to him noisily.

One calls to the young man atop the hill, "Octave, come see. Come play with us."

He answers in an authoritative voice. "This is a holy place, children. Leave the stones be. This is the place of the crosses."

Instantly their disappointment at a mild reproof becomes excitement at the prospect of an entertainment. "Is there a story, Octave? Tell us the story," they beg. All taking up the chant. He waves his hand and the staff to bid them be quiet as they race up the slope again and settle in a circle around him.

Pacing, he thinks he must tell them now, as his father had once told him. Tell them of another time of suffering, of oppression and death. Tell them of holding to hope even in pain. As young as they were, it was time. The children fell silent, looking up at him. He walked through the circle and crouching down, extended his arm and the staff as far as it would reach toward the setting sun. Tapping the ground once, he slowly raised the stick up over his head in an arc and then ran with it pointing straight up, through the circle again in the opposite direction. Spread-eagled, he stopped, carefully lowered it toward the dark distant mountains, and touched the earth. Then he repeated the ritual, running, the lance bobbing toward the heavens until it touched down where it had begun.

Back in their center again, the voice found him then. He began, "Once, there were Liberators ..."

So it is that ordinary men, through great sacrifice, become Legend.

Acknowledgments

For anyone wishing to pursue further study of the Eighth Air Force's history, I would recommend the works of Roger A. Freeman and the 392nd BG's Bob Vickers. In addition, British anthologist Ian Hawkins is a contributor to *20th Century Crusaders,* a compilation of the experiences of the men of the 392nd BG, edited by M.Sgt. Bill Braddock. Among the dozens of titles available, there is no finer detailed recreation of the life of a B24 crew in the final months of the war than *Wings of Morning,* by Thomas Childers. This is a remarkable and dedicated work.

As much as can be known and verified, the events depicted in this book are all true. In some instances, the personal thoughts, dialogue, and certain minor actions of individuals in 1943-44 are imagined based on the author's knowledge of the subjects and background provided to me. Combat accounts of participants and eyewitnesses often conflict, and those who survived the Friedrichshafen mission, and the war, are not in agreement on all details. Based on their accounts and the military record, I have done my best to give a continuous, coherent telling that is true to their recollections and is essentially fair to all. In this larger pursuit, it was never my intention to discredit, slight, or give offense to anyone.

Many people have supported my efforts to retrace my father's last steps and the development of this book. They are all, in a sense, co-authors and this is especially true of the veterans of the 392nd Bomb Group and the Eighth Air Force with whom I have been fortunate to associate. I am ever grateful to them for treating me like the "Air Force brat" I really am, one of their family. My thanks to all the facilitators mentioned in this book on both sides of the Atlantic, and especially to Jim Marsteller, Cliff Peterson, Mr. and Mrs. Michael Cugini, and my friend and fellow writer Hugh Malcolm Hinshaw.

My good friend Tun Aung created the front cover art design and two illustrations for this book. Bill May, Jr. did the overall design, while Julie Shissler prepared the book's layout. Jack Forgy and Lou Cox volunteered valuable technical assistance. I want to thank Maggie Laws, my publisher's intern, for her editing suggestions. My editor, Patty Wheeler, made this project come to fruition through her insight and creative effort. We will always share a special bond represented by this book, since she too lost her dad, Lieutenant Benjamin Nash, a submariner in WWII.

For resolutely standing by me and my aspirations, I also wish to thank all my dear friends in Larchmont, my hometown, and in particular Ray Messing and Nancy Manion. My father's family, my aunts and uncles, have been patient and understanding throughout the difficult process of exploring the past. I hope the final results will honor them.

My special thanks and appreciation to Renee Schmauss McGuire, my daughter-in-law, who diligently edited and word processed the text with me.

To all my immediate family, including the Navigator's grandchildren, their spouses, and his great grand children - I bow to you. And most of all, love and undying gratitude to my wife, Bernadette, who has been with me in the writer's life since I was a boy and has never stopped believing. Without her - for me - there would have been no story to tell.

Finally, for the thousands like me who lost their fathers and still feel the loss, my brothers and sisters, remember why and be proud.

"La coeur a ses raisons que la raison ne connait point."
The heart has reasons that reason knows nothing of.

W. C. McGuire II

Appendix
Information Sources

For those interested in attempting to gather information about the war dead and missing, the following is intended as a rudimentary listing of potential information sources. This list was compiled based on my experience and on the more comprehensive and instructive guide *Touchstones*, which is listed in the bibliography. This book was produced by the cofounder of the American World War II Orphans Network (AWON), Ann Bennett Mix. Members of this organization have also contributed to the list that follows.

AWON recommends beginning with the VA (Veterans Administration), which compiles files by name and can supply veterans' service numbers. With the service number in hand, inquiries may be made for the official Military Personnel file at the National Personnel Records Center (NPRC), St. Louis, and Mortuary Records.

Some records are available only to next of kin for veterans killed or missing in action. Some information may be obtainable to other than next of kin on the basis of a Freedom of Information Act request, but generally these will take considerably longer.

Your correspondence should always mention why you seek information and should include your relationship to the veteran and some proof of that relationship. For identification purposes, it should mention the relevant service number and social security number if available. Also include, if you know it, the military unit, group, outfit, etc. that he belonged to, and where possible, the date of death and location at that time.

Morning Reports from the date of death (from the NPRC) and the equivalent Naval and Marine Muster Rolls should also be requested for they can be a valuable source of information. Also ask for all supporting documents and for any documents used to reconstruct files. In the case of Army Air Force personnel who flew, Flight Records may also prove available.

Some of the web pages and other private sources listed below may charge for some services or use. Anything included here has proven informational value and that is my only criterion.

Don't be defeated if a record has been destroyed or is unavailable from any one agency. Often, though not always, the same material will exist with another agency. Quality of microfiche documents is also an issue, sometimes making copying or duplication poor to impossible. Some of your requests may take repeated and item-specific efforts, as well as months to answer. But patience, persistence, and a positive attitude will pay off over time. Best of all, as this book proves, one thing discovered and known will inevitably lead to another. Good luck. Keep 'em flying!

Department of Veterans Affairs (VA)
Phone 1-800-827-1000

Chief, Army Reference Branch
NCPMA-O
Military Personnel Records
National Personnel Records Center
9700 Page Blvd.
St. Louis, MO 63132-5100

Chief, HQ DA, Mortuary Affairs and Casualty Support Div.
Attention: DAPC-PED-F
Department of the Army
Re: IDPF-Individual Deceased Personnel File)
U.S. Total Army Personnel Command
2461 Eisenhower Ave.
(Hoffman Bldg. #1)
Alexandria, VA 22331-0482
Phone (703) 325-5300 Fax (703) 325-5315

Commanding Officer, Inquiries Branch/HQ AFHRA/RSQ
Air Force Historical Research Agency
600 Chennault Circle
Maxwell Air Force Base, AL 36112-6424
Phone (334) 953-2437 Fax (334) 953-4096
E-Mail afhranews1%rs%afhra@max1.au.af.mil

Chief, The National Archives At College Park
Archives II Textual Reference Branch NNR2
8601 Adelphi Road
College Park, MD 20740-6001
Phone (301) 713-7250 Fax (314) 538-4255

Attention: NNRM
(Foreign Records Seized)
National Archives
Washington, DC 20409

Edward A. Kueppers Jr., Information Manager
Eighth Air Force Historical Society
P.O. Box 7215
711 South Smith Ave.
Saint Paul, MN 55107

Director, The Mighty Eighth Air Force Museum
P.O. Box 1992
Savannah, Georgia 31402

American Battle Monuments Commission
Operations
Courthouse Plaza 2 – Suite 500
2300 Clarendon Blvd.
Arlington, VA 22201
Phone (703) 696-6897 Fax (703) 696-6666

Commanding Officer, Naval Medical and Dental Affairs
Mortuary Affairs Branch
P.O. Box 886999
Great Lakes, IL 60088-6999
Phone (800) 876-1131 Exts. 621, 627, or 628
Fax (847) 688-3964

Marine Corps Commandant
Code M-HP-10
HQ Marine Corps
2 Navy Annex
Washington, DC 20380-1775
Phone (703) 784-2121 Fax (703) 696-2072

Re: Marine Corps Records, National Archives
Archives II Textual Reference Branch NNR2
8601 Adelphi Rd.
College Park, MD 20740-6001
Phone (301) 713-7250 Fax (314) 538-4255

U.S. World War II Memorial Fund
American Battle Monuments Commission
Room 5127
20 Massachusetts Ave. NW
Washington, DC 20314-0001

National Guard records:
contact Adjutant General Office of the appropriate state

Ship Histories Branch Naval Historical Center
901 M St. SE
Washington, DC 20374-5060
Phone (202) 433-3643 Fax (202) 433-6677

For forwarding and address correction requested:

American Legion National Headquarters
Archiving and Researching Division/Personnel Tracking
> P.O. Box 1955
> Indianapolis, IN 46206
> Phone (317) 630-1200 Fax (317) 630-1241
> Web site: http://www.legion.org

Additional Veterans Information/Reunions
> Web site: http://www.vets.org
> Phone (573) 474-4444

Vets Tracing
> (Commercial Service – expensive)
> Phone: (800) 937-2133

For forwarding and address correction requested:

Veterans of Foreign Wars
> 404 West 34th St.
> Kansas City, MO 64111
> Phone (816) 756-3390 Fax (816) 968-1169

American WWII Orphans Network
> #910 Princess Anne Street
> Fredericksburg, VA 22401
> Phone (540) 310-0750 Fax (540) 310-0178
> E Mail awon@nas.com
> Web site http://www.awon.org

Additional Military Locators for the Living:

Air Force: HQAFMPC/MPCD 003
95041 H 35 North
San Antonio, TX 20593

Army:	Commander ARPCATTN:DARP-PAS-EVS 9700 Page Ave. St. Louis, MO 63132
Marine Corps:	CMCMMRB 10 HQ USAMC Bldg. 2008 Quantico, VA 22134-0001
Navy:	NPRC (Code 41) 4400 Dauphine St. New Orleans, LA 70149-7800
Coast Guard:	Coast Guard Commandant (G-PS-1) U.S. Coast Guard Locator 2100-2nd St. SW Washington, DC 20593
U.S. Merchant Marine:	Commandant U.S. Coast Guard (G-MVP-6) 2100 2nd St. SW Washington, DC 20593-001

National D-Day Museum
>Phone (504) 527-6012
>Eisenhower Center
>Phone (504) 539-9560
>923 Magazine St.
>New Orleans, LA 70130

Social Security Administration
Office of Central Records Operation
>300 North Green St.
>Baltimore, MD 21201
>Phone 1-800-772-1213

Additional Web Site Resources

Second Air Div. Assn., Eighth Air Force
http://www.ecn.co.uk/memorial/index.htm

U.S. Air Force Museum at Wright-Patterson Air Force Base
http://www.wpafb.af.mil/museum/index.html

B24 Web Page
http://www.mach3ww.com/B24

Aviation Archaeology
http://www..bogo.co.uk/air-research/aahome.htm

390ᵗʰ BG Memorial Museum
www.390ᵗʰ.org

392ⁿᵈ BG (Memorial Association)
www.b24.net

The Pacific Wreck Database
http://www.mhv.net/~wanpela/wrecks/

Army Air Corps, Veterans Information
http://www.army.mil/vetinfo/af.cfm

Army Air Corps, Contacts and Newsletters
http://www.army.mil/vetinfo/af.htm

Planes and Pilots of WWII
http://home.att.net/~C.C.Jordan/index.html

WWII Webring
http:www.webring.org/cgi-bin/webring?=ww2;list

Select Bibliography

Flight Manual for B-24 Liberator (Appleton, WI: Aviation Publications, 1989, 1942)

Ardery, Philip, *Bomber Pilot: A Memoir of World War II* (Lexington, KY: University Press of Kentucky, 1978)

Astor, Gerald, *The Mighty Eighth: The Air War in Europe as Told by the Men Who Fought It* (New York: D. I. Fine Books, 1997)

Bailey, Mike (with Tony North), *Liberator Album: B24 Liberators of the 2nd Air Division USAAF* (Leicester, England: Midland Publishing, 1998).

Bendiner, Elmer, *The Fall of Fortresses: A Personal Account of the Most Daring, and Deadly, American Air Battles of World War II* (New York: Putnam, 1980)

Bowman, Martin W., *The B-24 Liberator, 1939-1945* (Norwich, Wensum, England: 1979; Chicago, IL: Rand McNally, 1980)

Bowman, Martin W., *USAAF Handbook 1930-1945* (Mechanicsburg, PA: Stackpole Books, 1997)

Braddock, Bill and Marge Braddock (ed.), *Twentieth Century Crusaders: 392nd Bombardment Group (H)* (Paducah, KY: Turner Publishing Co., 1997)

Childers, Thomas, *Wings of Morning* (Reading, MA: Addison-Wesley, 1995)

Crosby, Harry H., *A Wing and a Prayer: The "Bloody 100th" Bomb Group of the U.S. Eighth Air Force in Action Over Europe in World War II* (New York: Harper Paperbacks, 1993)

Deighton, Len, *Blood, Tears, and Folly: An Objective Look at World War II* (New York: Harper Perennial, 1994)

Deighton, Len, *Goodbye, Mickey Mouse* (New York: Alfred A. Knopf, 1982)

Doolittle, Gen. James H. "Jimmy", *I Could Never Be So Lucky Again* (New York: Bantam Books, 1991)

Freeman, Roger A., *Experiences of War: The American Airmen in Europe* (Osceola, WI: Motorbooks International, 1991)

Freeman, Roger A., *The Mighty Eighth: A History of the Units, Men and Machines of the U.S. 8th Air Force* (London, Macdonald, 1970; Osceola, WI: Motorbooks International, 1991)

Freeman, Roger A. (with Alan Crouchman and Vic Maslen), *The Mighty Eighth War Diary*, (Osceola, WI: Motorbooks International, 1981)

Hadler, Susan and Ann Bennett Mix, *Lost in the Victory: Reflections of American Orphans of World War II* (Denton, TX: University of North Texas Press, 1998)

Jablonski, Edward, *America in the Air War* (Alexandria, VA: Time-Life Books, 1982)

Kaplan, Philip and Jack Currie, *Round the Clock: The Experience of the Allied Bomber Crews who Flew by Day and by Night from England in the Second World War* (New York: Random House, 1993)

Mix, Ann Bennett, *Touchstones: A Guide to Records, Rights and Resources for Families of American WWII Casualties* (Bountiful, UT: AGLL, Inc., 1996)

Perkins, Paul et al., *The Soldier: Consolidated B-24 Liberator* (Charlottesville, VA: Howell Press, 1994)

Verrier, Anthony, *The Bomber Offensive* (London: B.T. Batsford Ltd, 1968)

Vickers, Col. Robert E., *The Liberators from Wendling: The Combat Story of the 392ⁿᵈ Bombardment Group (H) of the Eight Air Force during World War Two* (Albuquerque, NM: Unit Memorial Collection (392ⁿᵈ BG), 1977; Manhattan, KS:Sunflower University Press, 1987)

Vickers, Col. Robert E., *Remembrance of the Missing* (edited by Keith Roberts) (Manhattan, KS: Sunflower University Press, 1996 and 1998)

Video Recordings

B-24s At War: Series II (Warren, MI: American Sound & Video Corporation, 1980, 1989) (1 cassette, b&w)

Behind the Wire -- Allied Airmen in German Captivity (Produced by The 8ᵗʰ Air Force Historical Society, Producer: A. Allen Zimmerman) (Cronograph, Inc., 1996) (1 cassette, b&w)

Start Engines -- Plus 50 Years: A First Person History of the Eighth Air Force in World War II (Writer/Producer: A. Allen Zimmerman) (St. Paul, MN: The 8ᵗʰ Air Force Historical Society, 1991) (1 cassette)

Index

192

193

196